# The Ultimate Washington Bucket List

## The Most recent guide to the journey beyond the Beaten path

**Andrew Mellor**

# Copyright © 2024  Andrew Mellor

*Table of Contents*

# Chapter 1: Introduction to Washington State

Washington State, located in the Pacific Northwest of the United States, is a place where contrasts unite to produce a harmony as diverse as its scenery. My first interaction with Washington came from the stories my grandfather told. He frequently mentioned the towering Cascade Mountains, where peaks like Mount Rainier rise majestically, etching their icy silhouettes against the sky. He vividly remembered the Olympic Peninsula's lush, green expanse, a monument to nature's unrivaled splendor.

His stories depicted a state that was not only beautiful but also culturally and historically significant.

The heart of Washington is unquestionably Seattle, a city as well-known for its technological breakthroughs as it is for its iconic Space Needle. This bustling metropolis combines urban sophistication and natural grandeur. In the morning, one can meander through the historic Pike Place Market, sipping on a cup of locally roasted coffee, and then spend the afternoon visiting the tech-savvy areas, where the future appears to be unfolding before your eyes.

To properly grasp Washington, one must go beyond the city limits. The state's diversified topography includes the Olympic National Park's rainforests and jagged coastline, as well as the Palouse's arid, rolling hills. Each location has its tale, from the Native American tribes that initially inhabited this land to the pioneers who eventually moved here.

Washington is also a state that embraces cultural diversity, as evidenced by its food, art, and festivals. The culinary scene reflects its diverse population, with options ranging from authentic Asian cuisine to fresh seafood from the Pacific. Eastern

Washington's wineries and apple orchards offer a quieter but equally rich experience.

Washington State is more than just a location on a map. It is a mix of natural wonders, creative vitality, and cultural diversity. It's a place where previous stories meet future possibilities, inviting you to explore, discover, and create your own stories.

Washington State, sometimes known as Washington or the Evergreen State, offers a mix of natural beauty, dynamic urban hubs, and a diverse cultural tapestry. It is situated in the Pacific Northwest region of the United States, bordered by the Pacific Ocean to the west, Oregon to the south, Idaho to the east, and the Canadian province of British Columbia to the north.

The Cascade Mountain Range divides Washington into two different regions. To the west of the Cascades, the climate is generally maritime, with moderate, wet winters and chilly, dry summers. This region includes the thriving city of Seattle, which is recognized for its technology industry, music culture, and landmarks such as the Space Needle and Pike Place Market. The region is distinguished by its lush, deep woods, rough shoreline, and the breathtaking Olympic Peninsula.

East of the Cascades, the climate changes to arid, semi-desert conditions. This region is famous for its agriculture, particularly the production of apples, cherries, and wine. The terrain here is significantly different, with rolling hills, arid grasslands, and important river valleys such as the Columbia River. Spokane and the Tri-Cities (Kennewick, Pasco, and Richland) serve as the region's major cities, each providing a unique cultural and recreational experience.

Washington is an economic powerhouse, noted for its technology sector, which is focused in the Seattle area and includes giants such as Microsoft and Amazon.
The state also boasts a robust aerospace industry, led by Boeing, and a sizable agriculture sector, particularly in Eastern Washington. The state's economy benefits from its ports, particularly the Port of Seattle, which is a significant gateway for trade with Asia.

Culturally, Washington is as diverse as its terrain. It has a strong Native American heritage, a thriving arts scene, and a past defined by exploration, creativity, and immigration. The state is noted for its environmental consciousness, which reflects its citizens' strong connection to the natural world around them.

To summarize, Washington State is a microcosm of the Pacific Northwest's beauty and dynamism, offering a distinct blend of natural splendors, economic vibrancy, and a diversified cultural landscape.

# Cultural and Geographic Diversity

Washington State's cultural and geographic diversity is critical in creating a broad and diversified bucket list for any visitor or resident. This diversity is reflected not just in the state's landscapes, which span from coastal beaches to alpine peaks, but also in the rich tapestry of cultures that have impacted its history and present.

**Geographic Diversity:**
**1. Coastal activities:** The rough Pacific coastline provides spectacular views and unique activities, such as beachcombing in Olympic National Park and whale viewing in the San Juan Islands.
**2. Mountain Adventure:** The Cascade and Olympic mountain ranges offer numerous options for hiking, skiing, and mountaineering. Mountain peaks such as Mount Rainier and Mount St. Helens are must-see sites for any outdoor enthusiast.

**3. Arid Landscape:** Eastern Washington, with its semi-arid climate, is a dramatic contrast to the West. The rolling hills of the Palouse and the wineries of Yakima and Walla Walla Valley provide unique visual beauty and agricultural wealth.

**Cultural Diversity:**

**1. Indigenous Heritage:** The state has a considerable Native American population, including tribes such as the Makah, Spokane, and Yakima, which contribute to its rich heritage. Exploring tribal museums and cultural institutions should be on any cultural enthusiast's itinerary.

**2. Urban Culture:** Cities such as Seattle and Tacoma combine contemporary culture and heritage. Seattle's music scene, technological breakthroughs, and diversified culinary environment are a reflection of Washington's multicultural mix.

**3. Historical Sites:** From the Lewis and Clark Trail to historic pioneer villages, Washington's past is firmly ingrained in its present. Exploring these locations provides insight into the state's past.

**Implications for Bucket Lists:**
- A comprehensive Washington bucket list should contain both natural and cultural experiences.

- Activities include hiking in the Cascades, seeing the vineyards of Eastern Washington, and experiencing the rich art and music scenes in its cities.
- Understanding the impact of Native American civilizations, as well as the state's significance in American history and modern innovation, enhances every visit.

To summarize, Washington's cultural and geographic diversity is not just an aspect of its terrain, but also a key component of the experiences it provides. It enables a Washington bucket list to be both a tour across diverse natural beauties and a deep dive into a melting pot of cultural influences.

# Travel Tips and Best Times to Visit

Traveling to Washington State provides a wide range of experiences due to its unique climate and topography. Here are some travel ideas and insights into the best time to visit:

**Best Time to Visit:**
**1. Spring (April-June):** Enjoy milder weather and see the cherry blossoms in Washington, D.C. The

Skagit Valley Tulip Festival in April is an absolute must-see.

**2. Summer (July–August):** Ideal for outdoor activities such as hiking, camping, and exploring national parks. Long, sunny days are ideal for exploring Seattle and other urban places.

**3. Fall (September-November):** Enjoy the stunning fall color, particularly in the Cascade Mountains. It is also an excellent season for wine tasting in areas such as Yakima Valley.

**4. snow (December-March):** Ideal for snow sports enthusiasts. The mountains provide excellent ski and snowboarding opportunities. Be prepared for shorter days and rain, especially on the west side.


**Travel Tip:**

**1. Prepare for the Weather:** Western Washington has a lot of rain, so bring waterproof apparel. Eastern Washington can be extremely hot in the summer and frigid in the winter.

**2. Explore Beyond Seattle:** While Seattle is a popular destination, regions such as the Olympic Peninsula, Spokane, and the San Juan Islands provide distinct experiences.

**3. Transportation:** It is recommended that you rent a car to explore areas outside of the main cities.

Within cities, public transportation is reliable, particularly in Seattle.

**4. Stay Connected:** For visitors from outside the United States, consider purchasing a local SIM card for easier travel and communication.

**5. Enjoy Local Cuisine:** Washington is famous for its seafood, apples, berries, and craft beer. Don't pass up the opportunity to try fresh, local produce.

**6. Respect Nature:** When hiking or camping, follow the Leave No Trace guidelines to protect the state's natural beauty.

**7. Cultural Events:** Check local calendars for festivals and events that may provide unique experiences, such as music festivals, art displays, and cultural festivities.

**8. Accommodation:** Make reservations in advance, especially during busy tourist seasons and around major festivals or events.

Washington State provides a rich tapestry of activities throughout the year, catering to a diverse variety of interests, from urban exploration to wilderness adventures. You may ensure a memorable and enjoyable vacation by planning accordingly for the season and following these travel guidelines.

*I Hope you are enjoying the book? In the paperback version of this book,you get access to a 10free travel Journal.*

# Chapter 2: Iconic Landmarks and Historical Sites

## *Seattle's Space Needle*

The Space Needle, an architectural marvel and Seattle emblem, is one of Washington State's most well-known landmarks. Originally built for the 1962 World's Fair, it has since become synonymous with the city's skyline. Towering at 605 feet, the Space Needle provides stunning views of the surrounding metropolis, mountains, and waterways, making it a must-see location for anybody visiting Seattle.

**Architectural Significance:**
**1. Design and Construction:** Inspired by the Space Age, its futuristic design reflected 1960s architects' vision of the future. The structure's distinctive design, which was commonly compared to a flying saucer, was revolutionary at the time.
**2. Renovations and Innovations:** The Space Needle has undergone multiple renovations to improve the tourist experience, including the installation of a spinning glass floor and

floor-to-ceiling glass viewing panels, which provide unobstructed panoramic views.

**Visitor Experience:**

**1. The Observation Deck:** At 520 feet, the observation deck offers 360-degree views of the Seattle skyline, Mount Rainier, the Olympic and Cascade Mountains, and Puget Sound.

**2. The Loupe Lounge:** Experience the thrill of walking on the world's first and only revolving glass floor, which provides a unique view of the city below.

**3. SkyCity Restaurant:** Although temporarily closed, it is still an iconic component of the Space Needle experience, providing eating with a view.

**Cultural and Recreational Aspects:**

**1. Photographic Landmark:** The Space Needle is a photographer's dream, offering breathtaking views of the city and surroundings.

**2. Events & Celebrations:** It hosts a variety of events, including the New Year's Eve fireworks, making it an important element of Seattle's cultural traditions.

**Why This Is a Bucket List Item:**

The Space Needle is more than just an observation tower; it represents innovation and forward thinking. Its distinctive design, history, and breathtaking vistas make it an important element of the Seattle experience. The Space Needle is a must-see location for anyone interested in architecture, enjoys spectacular vistas, or wants to immerse themselves in Seattle culture.

To summarize, the Space Needle is more than just an observation tower; it is a celebration of invention and a symbol of Seattle's vitality. Visiting this historic monument provides a fascinating experience that combines stunning vistas, architectural genius, and a strong connection to the city's culture, earning a position on any Washington State bucket list.

## *The State Capitol in Olympia*

The State Capitol in Olympia, the heart of Washington's political environment, is more than just a legislative hotspot. This stately edifice, located on the Washington State Capitol Campus, represents the state's rich history and architectural magnificence. It's a must-see for anybody visiting Washington, providing a mix of educational activities, breathtaking views, and a deep dive into the state's governance.

**Architectural and Historical Significance:**
**1. Design and Construction:** Built in 1928, the Capitol Building, also known as the Legislative Building, is a stunning example of Georgian Neoclassical architecture. It has a magnificent dome, one of the tallest brick domes in the world.
**2. Art and Decor:** The interior is similarly stunning, featuring Tiffany chandeliers, exquisite mosaics, and hand-carved woodwork embellishments.
**3. The Tivoli Fountain:** This landmark on the Capitol grounds, modeled after a fountain in Tivoli, Italy, is a popular attraction among visitors.

**Visitor Experience:**
**1. Guided Tours:** Free guided tours are given, providing information on the building's history, architecture, and legislative procedure.
**2. Self-Guided Explorations:** Visitors can also take self-guided tours and explore at their speed.
**3. Capital Campus:** Other significant buildings on campus include the Temple of Justice and the Governor's Mansion, both of which are placed in beautifully landscaped gardens.

**Cultural and educational aspects:**
**1. Legislative Sessions:** Visitors can see the legislature in session and obtain firsthand knowledge of state government.

**2. Educational activities:** The Capitol offers a variety of educational activities, making it an excellent destination for students and history buffs.

**3. activities and Celebrations:** The campus organizes a variety of public activities, including concerts, rallies, and holiday parties.

**Why This Is a Bucket List Item:**

Visiting the State Capitol in Olympia is critical for understanding Washington's political history and architectural grandeur. It provides a unique blend of educational value, aesthetic appeal, and insight into the workings of state government. Whether you enjoy architecture, history, or the political process, the Capitol offers an enriching experience that embodies the essence of Washington.

Finally, the State Capitol in Olympia is a testimony to Washington's history and governance, making it a must-see for anybody traveling the Evergreen State.

## Historical Pioneer Square

Pioneer Square, in the heart of Seattle, Washington, is a district rich in history and culture. Known as Seattle's original downtown, it was rebuilt following the Great Seattle Fire of 1889. Today, it is a bustling sector where the city's past and current intersect.

**Historical Significance:**

**1. Foundation of Seattle:** Pioneer Square was founded by Seattle's early residents in the 1850s.

**2. Architectural marvels:** Following the 1889 fire, the area was reconstructed in the great Romanesque Revival style. The region is today well-known for its old buildings made of brick and stone, with ornate facades and elaborate cornices.

**3. Underground Tour:** The Seattle Underground Tour provides a unique look at the city's history. It leads visitors through underground subterranean corridors that were formerly the main streets and businesses of historic Seattle.

**Cultural Aspects:**

1. Pioneer Square has a vibrant arts scene, with galleries and art walks featuring local and international artists.

**2. Native American Influence:** The district also reflects Native American culture, as evidenced by several public artworks and indigenous-themed galleries.

**3. gastronomic Delights:** The area has a variety of restaurants and cafes that serve everything from gourmet meals to informal eats, demonstrating the region's gastronomic diversity.

**Activities and Attractions:**

1. Visit the historic Smith Tower Observatory and enjoy panoramic views of Seattle and its surroundings.

**2. Klondike Gold Rush National Historical Park:** This park provides information about the impact of the Gold Rush on Seattle's growth.

**3. Occidental Square:** Experience the lively public space famed for its art installations, enormous chess set, and regular community events.

**Why This Is a Bucket List Item:** Pioneer Square is a must-see for anybody interested in Seattle's rich history. Its combination of rich history, architectural beauty, cultural diversity, and dynamic urban life makes it an essential visit on any Washington State itinerary. Whether you're a history buff, an art enthusiast, or simply someone who enjoys the distinct character of historic city areas, Pioneer Square provides an amazing experience.

# Mount St. Helens National Volcanic Monument

Mount St. Helens, a stratovolcano in Washington's Cascade Range, is most known for its catastrophic eruption on May 18, 1980. This catastrophe transformed the landscape and changed the environment, prompting the establishment of the Mount St. Helens National Volcanic Monument in 1982. This 110,000-acre region dedicated to study, recreation, and teaching provides a one-of-a-kind opportunity to explore a landscape profoundly altered by volcanic activity.

**Geological Significance:**
**1. Eruption of 1980:** The eruption, one of the most powerful in U.S. history, inflicted widespread devastation and significantly altered the landscape. The bomb zone is visible today.
**2. Regeneration & Research:** The area is used as a natural laboratory to investigate ecological and geological change. The restoration and recovery of flora and wildlife reveal fascinating details about nature's resilience.

**Visitor Experience:**

**1. Johnston Ridge Observatory:** Provides breathtaking views of the crater, explanatory displays, and instructional films about the eruption and aftermath.

**2. Hiking routes:** Several routes, including the Hummocks Trail and the Lava Canyon Trail, provide hikes of varied complexity that highlight the area's geological features and recovery.

**3. Climbing the top:** Permits are available for ambitious climbers to Mount St. Helens' top, which offers a demanding hike and beautiful vistas.

**Cultural and Educational Aspects:**

**1. Educational Centers:** Visitor centers near the monument offer detailed information on the volcano's history, geology, and ecology.

**2. Guided Tours:** Ranger-led programs and guided walks are provided, providing further information about the monument's significance and the natural recovery process.

**Why This Is a Bucket List Item:**

Mount St. Helens National Volcanic Monument demonstrates not only nature's raw strength but also its incredible ability to heal and rejuvenate. It combines natural beauty, geological intrigue, and educational value. Mount St. Helens offers a compelling and remarkable experience for anyone who enjoys the outdoors, is interested in science, or is simply amazed by the forces of nature.

Finally, the Mount St. Helens National Volcanic Monument serves as a poignant reminder of both nature's instability and ongoing endurance. A visit here is required for anyone interested in experiencing the awe-inspiring force of volcanoes as well as witnessing the incredible processes of ecological recovery and regeneration, making it an important addition to any Washington State bucket list.

# Chapter 3: Natural Wonders and Outdoor Adventures

## *Hiking in Olympic National Park*

### Getting home from Olympic National Park

The nearest major airport, Seattle-Tacoma International Airport (SEA), is two and a half hours from Port Angeles, the core of the Olympics.

To reach Port Angeles, we recommend taking a ferry from Seattle to Bremerton. This route provides a fantastic perspective of the Seattle skyline from the boat, is a fun way to travel, and allows you to avoid traffic on I-5. If you're coming from the Portland area, take Highway 101 for the greatest views. The best way to experience the Olympic Peninsula is to explore the park by car.

### National Park Pass

You will also need to get a parking pass. The America the Beautiful Pass is valid for a year and includes admission to all national parks, or you can purchase a seven-day pass to Olympic National Park.

Passes can be purchased at the Olympic National Park Visitor Center in Port Angeles, park entrances at Hurricane Ridge, the Hoh Rainforest, Sol Duc, and Staircase, online, or at REI Seattle.

**The best time to visit**
Our favorite aspect of the Olympics is that most of it is open year-round. When to visit is entirely up to personal preference!

Summer (ideal for weather and trekking)
July — September
Summer temperatures can reach the low 70s throughout the year, as the environment is always moderate. By July, you'll have a variety of high-elevation excursions to select from, and all routes will be free of snow. This is the best time to visit the park if you want to avoid rain and walk in the mountains.

Ruby Beach during a lovely weekend in September.

Fall (ideal for waterfalls)
October — November
With more rain — an average of 10 days per month — fall is an excellent season to visit the Olympics.

There are fewer tourists, though some seasonal highways may close beginning in mid-November.

Winter (ideal for crowds)
December - March
Most tourists avoid the Olympics during the winter due to a fear of rain. However, the amount of rain you can expect varies substantially by region. The village of Forks, near the Hoh Rainforest, is North America's wettest spot. They get up to 10 feet of rain each year (approximately 20 days of rain per month during the winter), whereas locations like Port Angeles get 12 days of rain in the winter.

Temperatures at lower elevations are typically in the 40s throughout the region, and gloomy skies provide the dramatic landscapes that the Pacific Northwest is known for.

Here in Washington, we believe that there is no such thing as terrible weather, only bad wardrobe choices, so take a raincoat (see our packing list below) and waterproof shoes such as hiking or rain boots. Don't be frightened to visit in the winter!

Spring (ideal for flora and waterfalls).
February — June
The trees become especially lush as the winter melts, and waterfalls begin to erupt in the spring.

There is still a risk of a few wet days during your vacation, but temps should range from the 50s to 60s.

# Where to Stay?

**Port Angeles**
Port Angeles is the core of the Olympic National Park. Its central location means that many bucket-list sites are only an hour's drive away. It also borders Washington's rain shadow, therefore it gets far less rain than the Olympic National Park's western side. It is also the largest town in the area, so you will have the most options for restaurants and lodging.

**Olympic Railway Inn: Pet-friendly train cars, sleeps 2-4.**
**Starlight Camp:** Glamping tents, sleeps 2-4.
**Juan De Fuca Cottages:** Waterfront Cabins – Sleeps 5-8
**Eagles Landing:** Beautiful historic cabin feel with hot tub—sleeps 10
**Lavender Castle:** Pet-friendly castle, with hot tub—sleeps **12**

**Lake Crescent / Lake Sutherland**
These lakes are located half an hour west of Port Angeles. The location has few amenities but makes up for it with beauty.

**Lake Crescent Lodge:** An Olympic National Park Lodge on the lake, beds 2-4.

**Log Cabin Resort:** Olympic National Park cottages at Lake Crescent, beds 2-4.

**Lake Sutherland Waterfront:** Includes kayaks and a hot tub — sleeps four

**Rustic Lakefront Cabin:** On Lake Sutherland, complete with your dock— sleeps six.

**Lake Sutherland Waterfront Home with Hot Tub and Views — Sleeps 12.**

## Sol Duc

Home to the Olympic Peninsula's only commercial hot springs. The lodge and hot springs are open periodically, from late March until October.

**Sol Duc Hot Springs is an Olympic National Park Lodge located in the wilderness that can accommodate groups of 2 to 10.**

## Forks

Forks is an excellent home base for exploring the coast and the Hoh rainforest. The town is small, with few services, but the surrounding forests and beaches are stunning. Even after all these years, the town still clings to its Twilight famous, therefore related items can be found all across town.

**Dew Drop Inn Motel:** centrally located in town, sleeps 2-4.

**Misty Valley Inn B&B:** Serene setting with breakfast included, beds 2-4.

**Peaceful Retreat:** 10 acres with a historic log cabin that sleeps eight.

**Private home:** Spacious home on acreage — sleeps eleven.

## Neah Bay

Neah Bay is worth visiting, however, it is somewhat remote. If you have time, stay close and appreciate how remote this part of Washington is.

**Chito Beach Resort:** Private waterfront villas, 20 minutes from Neah Bay — sleeps 1–2.

**Hobuck Beach Resort:** Beachfront Cabins Near Neah Bay, Sleeps 2-6

## Kalaloch

The Olympic National Park Lodge is located between Forks and Lake Quinault. It is popular, so you must be lucky to secure a reservation, but it is the ideal beach vacation.

**Kalaloch Lodge:** cute cabins, a lodge, and campsites—sleeps 2-4

**Lake Quinault**

Another national park lodge, quaint private cottages, and one of our favorite campgrounds (more on that below) line the lake.

**Lake Quinault Lodge:** An Olympic National Park Lodge on the lake, beds 2-4.
**Locharie chalets:** Waterfront chalets, beds 2-6.
**Secluded Lakefront Retreat: Gorgeous Home and Views – Sleeps 6.**
**Lake Cushman/Hoodsport**

Hoodsport is a charming village on the Puget Sound. Stay there for easy access to eateries, or visit Lake Cushman and kayak right from your front.

**Hoodsport Home:** Bright and charming seaside home, that sleeps three.
**Waterfront at Hoodsport:** Octagonal villa with ocean views and dock—sleeps four
**Lake Cushman Home:** Spacious, with patio, dock, and kayaks—sleeps 6
**Lake Hideaway:** Forest paradise on Lake Cushman with gaming room—sleeps ten

**Port Townsend**

Port Townsend, a Victorian seaport, is a historic beauty. The town is enjoyable to explore, highly walkable, boasts a historic World War II Fort, excellent food, and easy access to ferries.

**The Adams Pragge House Bed & Breakfast:** Very Victorian, in a historic neighborhood, beds two.

**Tides Inn & Suites:** Modern waterfront motel in historic downtown; sleeps 2-4.

**Port Townsend Cottage** – Retreat outside of town - sleeps four.

**Bishop Hotel:** Modern, yet still Victorian hotel in historic downtown, beds 2-6.

## Camping
Camping is a fantastic way to experience the Olympics! Many of the sites allow RVs, vans, and tents. Campgrounds tend to fill up quickly, so we recommend booking your spot as soon as it goes on sale. We find it easier to find a campsite between the fall and spring.

Our favorite campgrounds so far are Willaby Campground, Kalaloch, Staircase, Salt Creek Recreation Area, the Wild WA Coast Lookout, Jardin du Soleil Lavender Farm, and Robert Woods.

## Campground rentals
If you're going from out of state or don't have camping gear, consider renting it from Backcountry 40 Outfitters, a Seattle-based firm, or REI.

If you like exploring in a van, look at Indie Campers and Escape Campervans.

## Hiking

The Olympic National Park has plenty of renowned trails! There are approximately 135 miles of trails, and each part of the park is distinct from the others. We appreciate that the walks in the lowlands are accessible year-round. We'll give specific hike recommendations in the itinerary below.

## Best Activities

Ranger-led programs
Check the park schedule for information on guided walks, art exhibits, and Hurricane Ridge's telescope program.

## Tide pooling

Before looking for tide pools, make sure to check the tide chart. We enjoy utilizing tides.net since they provide tidal charts and a graph.

Wear a decent pair of waterproof hiking boots or rain boots to the tidal pool (product links are included in our packing list). The areas around the tide pools are rough, and your shoes will most certainly become wet. Going barefoot is not an ideal option for this sport.

Be aware that more than one low tide may occur in a single day. If this is the case, the second low tide is unlikely to be extremely low, making tide pooling difficult.

**Important:** remember when the tide begins to rise – it's easy to become concerned about spotting animals, and you don't want to end up stranded on a high piece of beach. Pay attention to the time and know when the tide will start to rise. Keep a watch out for sneaker waves, too!

### Paddling

Most lakes in Olympic National Park are suitable for kayaking and paddleboarding. Seasonal rentals are provided at Lake Cushman at Skokomish Park, Lake Quinault at the Lake Crescent Lodge, and Hoodsport Wellness and Kayak Rentals.

### Lavender Farms

Sequim (near Port Angeles) is rich in lavender farms. They're usually open from May to October and sell things like you-pick lavender, lavender products, and even lavender-flavored ice cream.

**Check out this list to find the best farm to visit on your trip.**

**Crab fest**
Every year in October, Port Angeles hosts Crab Fest for one weekend. Purchase tickets for a Dungeness crab meal, or attend the free festival.

**Farmers' Market.**
Port Angeles hosts a year-round farmers market with delicious cuisine and a variety of crafts. It may be found near the Gateway Transit Center Pavillion downtown. Stop by Welly's Real Fruit Ice Cream (New Zealand style) while you're around!

## Hurricane Ridge
**Summer**
This location, about an hour from Port Angeles, offers stunning mountain views. It's an excellent place to observe the sunrise or sunset because of the panoramic views from the parking lot.

Although trekking is not required to appreciate the views here, it does allow you to spend more time taking in the scenery. Check out Sunrise Point for a fast hike, Hurricane Hill and Klahhane Ridge for longer hikes, or Mount Angeles for a class 3 scramble.

Unfortunately, a fire destroyed the Hurricane Ridge Day Lodge in the spring of 2023. The park has reopened Hurricane Ridge to a restricted number of tourists each day. We recommend coming before

10:00 a.m. before they reach maximum capacity and close for the day.

**Winter**
Hurricane Ridge is only open Friday through Sunday from late November to late March (depending on snow depth). The route opens on these days once the plows have cleared the roadways, which might be as early as 8 a.m. or as late as noon, depending on the conditions.

**Hurricane Hill**
Having chains in or on your car is needed during these months. We recommend purchasing chains from Les Schwab Tire Centers since they will let you return them if they are unused.

Because parking is limited at the summit, the lot fills up quickly. After that, cars are let in one at a time while others leave. Arrive at 7 a.m. to secure an early spot in line; otherwise, you may face a one-to three-hour wait.

Once you've arrived, there's a tiny sledding hill (bring your sleds), ranger-led snowshoes, or you may snowshoe the Hurricane Hill track yourself. This trail is avalanche-prone. On days with low avalanche risk, you can snowshoe along the ridge to Hurricane Hill.
Stay away from the ridge's edge, which frequently has cornices that can cause you to fall through. On days with moderate to high avalanche risk, walk through the lower meadows.

## Olympic National Park Itineraries: 1–7 Days

This trip is quite active, with long drives, hiking possibilities, and gorgeous scenery. Follow it in the recommended sequence to see as much of the park as possible, or stay longer in one of the towns to explore more in one location.

If you only have seven days to explore, you'll need to decide where to cut this schedule short based on the things you want to prioritize and the amount of drive time you're willing to spend returning to Seattle.

**Day 1's itinerary**

We're starting this itinerary in Seattle because traveling to the Olympic Peninsula is half the enjoyment. You'll end the day with a beautiful sunset!

**Mileage: 80.**
**Driving time: 2.5 hours.**
**Start in Seattle.**
**End: Port Angeles.**

**Click the link HERE to see the location on maps or Scan QR code with a device.**

**Ferry**
Take the ferry from downtown Seattle to Bainbridge Island. To get in line, arrive at the ferry port around 20 minutes before departure. You'll drive on, and once you've boarded, get out of the automobile and explore the boat! At the beginning of the journey, you'll have a magnificent view of the Seattle skyline. Don't worry about timing; the

captain will notify you when it's time to return to your vehicle and begin deboarding.

## Port Gamble

Stop in or just drive by; this is a historic logging town. It has maintained its attractiveness over the years, and the town's main street is especially charming. If you are hungry, visit the Café in the general shop.

## Hurricane Ridge

If the outlook is clear when you arrive in Port Angeles, make your way to Hurricane Ridge. whether the mountains are shrouded in clouds, postpone your visit until another day, or take a chance and see whether the clouds lift before you arrive. Conditions fluctuate drastically depending on the season, so read the Hurricane Ridge section before coming.

The trip from Port Angeles to the top of Hurricane Ridge takes about an hour. It's an excellent site for watching the sunset, with views of the Bailey mountain range to the south and the Strait of Juan de Fuca and Canada to the north.

## Tongue Point

If the weather at Hurricane Ridge isn't cooperating, visit Tongue Point in Salt Creek Recreation Area.

From the parking lot, walk the path to the ocean until you reach a steep set of stairs leading down to the rocky beach. At low tide, you can descend the stairs to a stony beach with tide pools. At high tide, you can watch the water swirl around the stairs. It's one of our favorite places to watch sunsets.

**Day 2 itinerary.**
We recommend going to Forks for your second day at the Olympics because there is so much to see on the route. If you'll be in the area for a limited period, consider making Port Angeles your home base and doing longer day trips to Forks and Neah Bay from there.

**Mileage: 80.**
**Drive time: two hours.**
**Start at Port Angeles.**
**End: Forks.**

Click the link HERE to see the location on maps or Scan QR code with a device.

## Madison Falls

Your first destination should be Madison Falls. It's only a short detour from the main road, and the 0.2-mile route is paved, flat, and the waterfall falls year-round.

## Lake Crescent

Your next stop will be Lake Crescent. The lake is a vibrant blue, encircled by mountains. It looks beautiful regardless of the weather.

If you want to hike here, stop at the Storm King Ranger Station. If you're looking for a workout, hike to Marymere Falls or Mount Storm King. There is more information available about this hike, so if you are interested, read about it here.

View of Lake Crescent from Mount Storm King at sunset

If you'd rather enjoy a leisurely view of the lake, head to Lake Crescent Lodge. There is one of the national park's lodges, an idyllic dock, and quieter pathways to explore through the forest.

If you have more time to explore in this area, we recommend taking the Spruce Railroad Trail to the Devil's Punchbowl. The walk is paved, and about a mile in, you'll come across the Devil's Punchbowl, an extremely gorgeous swimming hole.

**Sol Duc**
Proceed to the Sol Duc Resort next. The route here is open periodically from late March until October. It contains another national park lodge, commercial hot springs, woods, and waterfalls. While you're here, you can swim and climb to Sol Duc Falls.

**Forks**
You'll have accomplished a lot in Forks, so come back the next day!

**Day 3 itinerary**
Your third day at the Olympics will be filled with spectacular jungles and beaches. Begin in the rainforest and end the day on the beach at sunset.

**Mileage: 90 miles.**
**Driving time: 2.5 hours.**

**Start: Forks.**
**End: Forks.**
**Hoh Rainforest**

We recommend starting your day at the Hoh Rainforest. On weekends, the line to enter often backs up, so arrive before 10 a.m. to avoid a delay. Hike the famed Hall of Mosses trail and/or the less well-known Spruce Nature Trail. It's not only less traveled, but it also parallels the Hoh River, where you may see deer and elk!

Click the link HERE to see the location on maps or Scan QR code with a device.

**Forks**

Go back to Forks for lunch. We recommend Sully's Drive-In and D&K BBQ. While you're in town, visit the Forks Timber Museum and the Forks Chamber of Commerce, which is stocked with Olympic National Park and Twilight memorabilia.

**Beach**

Finally, finish your day with a sunset at the beach. For quick beach access, go to James Island View Point in La Push. If you want to tide pool, trek to Second Beach or the Hole in the Wall at Rialto Beach.

Before visiting any place, find out when the tide is lowest. The best tide pools can be found around Teahwhit Head on Second Beach and the Hole in the Wall at Rialto Beach, however, they are referred to as tide traps. Be alert to the incoming tide or you'll get stranded!

 Rialto Beach, near the Hole in the Wall.

**Day 4's itinerary**
The fourth day will be spent touring Neah Bay. Getting there is inconvenient no matter where you're coming from, but Forks is the closest town and is well worth the short trip. It is feasible to stay near Neah Bay, however accommodation is limited.

**Mileage: 80.**
**Drive time: two hours.**
**Start: Forks.**

**End: Forks.**
Click the link HERE to see the location on maps or Scan QR code with a device.

**Neah Bay**
We are grateful that the Makah Tribe welcomes travelers to their beautiful territories. To trek here, you must obtain a Makah Recreation Pass. They're available at most places in town, but if you have time, we recommend visiting the Makah Marina to see sea lions or the Makah

Museum to see 300-500-year-old antiquities while getting your Makah Pass.

### Cape Flattery

If you only take one hike in the area, make it this one. Cape Flattery is the northwesternmost point in the contiguous United States, and it feels like you're on the edge of the planet.

The journey includes boardwalks through coastal woodlands, numerous overlooks, and excellent possibilities to see wildlife. Watch for whale spouts in the distance, sea otters beneath the overlooks, and nesting seabirds. Bring a monocular like this one to make the most of your hike!

### Hobuck Beach

If you have time, visit Hobuck Beach. It's the closest place to hang out on a sandy beach because Cape Flattery lacks beach access. It's an excellent location for watching the sunset, swimming, or surfing (just bring your wetsuit!).

### Do you have any extra time here?

### Shi Shi Beach

Hike to the Point of Arches on Shi Shi Beach. Plan your hike around low tide to the tidal pool at the Point of Arches, or pack some munchies to grill over a fire on the beach. If there are no fire restrictions in the area, burn driftwood rather than forest wood (which is part of the ecology).

**Ozette Triangle**

The Ozette Triangle is a particularly fascinating walk. If possible, time your hike around low tide. If the tide is five feet or lower, you can stroll around the Wedding Rocks and see more than 40 petroglyphs.

They are 300-500 years old and were created by the people of Ozette Village in Cape Alva. The Makah Museum houses artifacts from this village.

**Day 5's itinerary**

This day will be crammed with attractions along the coast and at Lake Quinault. Start early to enjoy a more relaxing pace.

**Mileage: 70.**
**Drive time: two hours.**
**Start: Forks.**
**Finally, there is Lake Quinault.**

Click the link <u>HERE</u> to see the location on maps or
Scan QR code with a device.

### Ruby Beach

Ruby Beach is an excellent stop. To get to the beach, you'll need to walk down a short but steep hill. Visit Abbey Island during low tide to see the tide pools.

High tide at Ruby Beach.

## Kalaloch

As you head south, stop at the Kalaloch Big Cedar Nature Trail to see a massive 1,000-year-old tree. From there, proceed to Kalaloch Campground to locate the Tree of Life.

Park at the campground's day-use area and walk to the right, north along the beach. The Tree of Life is a short walk away.

## Northside Lake Quinault

You'll end the day at Lake Quinault. To begin your exploration of the Maple Glade Rainforest route, visit the Quinault Rain Forest Ranger Station. It is extremely similar to the Hoh Rainforest but without the tourists. Extend the hike by exploring the Kestner Homestead as well.

Following that, you can continue driving on the Quinault Rainforest Loop Drive or turn around and return to the main road the same way you came. If you take the loop route, it's a picturesque forest road with gravel and a few potholes, but it's normally well-maintained. This drive takes roughly 1.5 hours, and you'll view the same attractions listed below in reverse order. Although it is available year-round, please check the road conditions before driving.

**The south shore of Lake Quinault.**

Take a look at our waterfall tour. Before seeing Merriman and Bunch Falls, stop at Lake Quinault

Lodge and observe the world's largest Sitka spruce. Keep a watch out for elk on your way there; they frequently graze near the Elkhorn Ranch.

**Day 6's itinerary**
The road between Lake Quinault and Lake Cushman is very simple in comparison to what you'll have traveled through by this time. However, it is the shortest path from Lake Quinault to the east edge of Olympic National Park.

It should be noted that the forest route leading to the Olympic National Park near Lake Cushman is blocked from November to May. You may monitor the road's status here. There isn't much to do in this area during the winter, so if you're planning a visit, skip this spot or use it as a stopover on your way to another location.

**Mileage: 100 miles.**
**Drive time: two hours.**
**Start at Lake Quinault.**
**Lake Cushman is the final destination.**
Click the link HERE to see the location on maps or Scan QR code with a device.

### Hoodsport

You'll go from Lake Quinault to Hoodsport, a little village on Puget Sound. Locals dig for clams, mussels, and oysters all year, and you can eat them at the Hamma Hamma Oyster Saloon (excellent for groups, but make reservations ahead of time) or our favorite place, The Fjord Oyster Bank.

### Lake Cushman

Spend the day exploring the shores of Lake Cushman at Staircase Campground. Along the way, you'll come across picnic areas and kayak launches. Staircase Rapids is a somewhat flat and easy, yet spectacular, trail that follows the Skokomish River. If you're looking for a challenge and are coming between June and October, include summiting Mt. Ellinor on your itinerary.

Spend an additional day here to kayak the Puget Sound or Lake Kokanee using rentals from Hoodsport Wellness.

## Day Seven itinerary

On this leg of your journey, you'll head north on Highway 101, passing through Puget Sound and stopping at waterfalls along the way. Your excursion will conclude in Port Townsend, where you can catch a ferry back to the mainland.

**Mileage: 70.**
**Driving time: 1.5 hours.**
**Start with Lake Cushman.**
**End: Port Townsend.**

## Port Townsend

Port Townsend is a Victorian seaport and one of our favorite places to visit in Washington.

Enjoy seafood at Doc's Marina Grill, a trip to Fort Worden to see World War II fort ruins or a bath and sauna session.

Leave the Olympic Peninsula in the same way you arrived: via ferry. If you take the ferry from Port Townsend to Coupeville, you'll conclude the Cascade Loop route. If you're returning to Seattle, take a drive around Whidbey Island before boarding another ferry from Clinton to Mukilteo.

**Where do we go next?**
**Not finished exploring Washington?** Visit another national park while you're here! The route you take will change based on your destination.

**North Cascades**
Take the boat from Port Townsend to Coupeville, then head north on Whidbey Island and follow our Cascade Loop route from there.

**Mount Rainier**
Take off from the Olympic Peninsula, either from Lake Quinault or Hoodsport, for Mount Rainier.

**Seattle**
We urge that you avoid driving on I-5 around Olympia, Tacoma, Seattle, and Everett if possible. Taking a ferry to Seattle is the best (and most enjoyable) method to accomplish this.

**Leave no trace.**
The Olympic National Park has a very fragile environment. It's critical to observe the Leave No Trace principles. One of the simplest ways to accomplish this is to stay on pathways, avoid wildflower meadows, and avoid climbing fallen trees (which are part of the ecosystem).

**What to Pack**

On the Olympic Peninsula, you never know what to anticipate in terms of weather, so pack a variety of clothes. You should be prepared for rain, sunshine, and chilly weather, especially if you intend to spend time in the highlands or on the beaches - the weather may change quickly here! Always pack an extra layer for these outings.

If you plan to hike here between October and June, tennis shoes will not suffice. You'll need waterproof boots or rainboots to keep your feet from getting soaked on muddy terrain.

**If you're hiking, plan to bring the following with you:**

**Hiking boots (for men and women)**
**Hiking socks (men's and women's)**
**Hiking daypack (for men and women)**
**Raincoat (men's or women's)**
**Mid-layer (men's or women's)**
**Bug spray**
**Hiking poles (ideal for longer hikes and increased stability)**

**The following ten essentials:**
**Water**
**We enjoy utilizing HydraPak's water bladders.**

**Snacks like this:**

**Cliff bars**
**Lara bars (gluten-free)**
**Trail Mix (Gluten-Free)**
**Archer's Jerky (gluten-free)**
**Dried fruits such as mango, apricots, or apple chips (gluten-free)**
**Emergency Shelter**
**Firestarter**
**Multitool**
**First Aid Kit**
**Headlamp**
**Compass and Map**
**Sun hat (for men and women)**
**Sunscreen**
**Sunglasses**

The following goods are useful if you're coming between fall and spring or wish to explore during sunrise or dusk when temperatures might drop considerably.

**Warm hat.**
**Gloves**
**Base layer shirts (men's and women's)**
**Base layer bottoms (men's and women's)**
**Packable puffy coat (for men and women).**

**Other helpful things:**
**Rain boots (men's and women's).**
**Rainboots are ideal for tidal pooling, although hiking boots can also be useful.**
**Packable, quick-dry towel**
**Ideal for drying off after a walk on the beach.**
**Female Urinary Device**

This is a game-changer for hiking trails! Using one of these gadgets allows you to pee while standing up, which provides substantially more privacy than without one.

**Hand sanitizer**
**Body Glide**
**Use it wherever to avoid chafing.**
**Salt pills (caffeinated or non-caffeinated).**

**These are useful during strenuous hikes to replace electrolytes and salt.**

**Park tips**
**Gasoline stations**
Gas stations can be found in every town surrounding the Olympic National Park. Plan your stops because these places are scattered away. There are few electric car chargers near the Olympic National Park, therefore we recommend driving a gasoline-powered vehicle.

**Restaurants**

Restaurants can be found at the park's lodges as well as in the surrounding towns. Because communities are small, businesses often close early; plan your lunch and dinner stops ahead of time. Bring food and drinks to chew on between towns.

**Cell service**

The Olympic Peninsula has intermittent cell service. You will have service near towns but do not expect it between them. Load your GPS directions for the day from your motel while you have WIFI before departing for the day.

**Wildlife**

Look for deer and elk on or near the road when driving, especially around dawn and twilight.

They tend to blend into the surrounding scenery and are frequently seen standing in or racing across the road. If you encounter one on the side of the road, slow down since they can make unexpected movements and there may be others around.

**Exploring Mount Rainier**

Going to Seattle soon and wondering about a day trip to Mount Rainier. You have arrived at the correct location!

I love national parks and try to visit them whenever feasible. Some excellent examples:

A few months ago, I spent more than 8 hours on a bus to get there.

We're taking a road trip to Idaho this summer (from California), and you can bet we'll be stopping at a few. Crater Lake is a certainty.

I've been begging my hubby for a long time to take me to Utah (for the national parks, not skiing). Simply ask her. You've never encountered a Boy who is so enthusiastic about Utah before.

I got lost after driving 3 hours on a dirt road to find the entrance to Rocky Mountain National Park. Next time...

Secretly arranging a trip to Palm Springs later this year to spend a day or two in Joshua Tree.

Mt. Rainier Day Trip

With that considered, when I started planning my trip, I knew a brief visit to Mount Rainier was a no-brainer. Seeing and feeling the mountain was an absolute must for me. After searching the internet for day excursions from the city (because I couldn't drive alone), I came across a firm that not only specializes in small group tours but also offers cookies and wine. I knew I'd found my match for my day excursion to Mount Rainier from Seattle.

I was sold. It was that simple. Most people enjoy cookies, but I prefer mine.

I must say that the two-hour drive to Mt. Rainier went pretty quickly. The time on the bus was spent talking about travel and national parks (my favorite topics), getting to know the other group members, and listening to our naturalist speak about the mountain and its environment. And enjoying a delicious breakfast of handmade banana nut bread. (And then eat another slice.)

Day Trip to Mount

Rainier from Seattle: Mountain Out!

And before we had even officially arrived, this was our first look at the mountain.

Pretty amazing, huh? I'll let you look at it for a bit since I understand it's a lot to take in. My day excursion to Mount Rainier from Seattle was definitely off to a wonderful start!

Mount Rainier is the tallest peak in both Washington and the Pacific Northwest's Cascade Range.

It is regarded as one of the most dangerous volcanoes in the world!
On very clear days, the peak can be visible from Portland, Oregon, and Victoria, British Columbia.
According to John Muir, the view is best seen from below. That's not to say the view from the summit isn't breathtaking!
At almost 14,410 feet above sea level, the mountain is unmistakably a landmark in Washington's landscape. You will know when you see it. That is for sure.

And the sights became better as the day progressed. Iconic. Majestic. Grandiose. Trust me, those points of view are difficult to articulate. No words can properly express the feeling you get when you look up at it.

**Mt. Rainier Day Trip**

Mt. Rainier Day Trip

Simply look at that. No wonder 1.5-2 million people visit every year.

Throughout the day, we went on some short walks in the vicinity, all with stunning views of the mountain volcano. Did you realize Mt. Rainier is a volcano? I didn't. It last erupted in 1894, and another major eruption is expected soon.

All of the stunning views were complemented by explanations about how the mountain developed, and fascinating information about climbers attempting to ascend the mountain and wildlife in the vicinity.

**Snow Shoeing**
It's one thing to see the mountain from a distance, but it's another to hike/snowshoe on it. So naturally, we did exactly that. The views were breathtaking, and you could even see glacial ice in the distance on the mountain! It seemed like the clearest, iciest blue I'd ever seen. A snowmobile would be an excellent way to see the area. supplies a vast range of snow sporting equipment, so if you're looking for anything from boots to coats, they'd be an excellent place to start.

The trek wasn't too tough, and the snowshoes made crunching down in the snow much easier. "

**Hiking through the Lowland Forest**

Our guide was quite educated about the plants and creatures that live in the forest, and we learned a lot about each species and how they work in the park's ecosystem.

He could have talked for days about each species of tree in the park (for real), but he kept the group interested and avoided going into too much depth with irrelevant information. (Thanks, Eric!) No questions were left unanswered.

Evergreen conifers, including western hemlock and Douglas fir. A couple of names I'd never heard before, some of which reached as high as 200 feet in the sky.

I felt so little (in the greatest way) in the forest.

**Waterfalls**

Throughout the day, we traveled various small trails that led us directly to enormous gushing waterfalls. We were lucky because the waterfalls are best seen in early summer and fall when the snow melts and feeds the streams.

One of the most stunning waterfalls we visited was Christine Falls, named for one of Mount Rainier's earliest climbers.

Breakfast and Lunch Food! Yes, please. Fortunately, all meals were provided, as it would have been inconvenient to make the short trip to Pike Place at 7 a.m. If you don't already know, I'm not an early riser and scream at the world when I have to get up before daybreak. (Unless I'm... that's another story.)

Thick slices of banana nut bread, coffee, and tea were served, and that's when I started to wake up. We stopped a few minutes before the park to get acclimated with the day's plans and grab some refreshments. AND french press coffee. In the midst of nowhere. It's ridiculous in a good sense.

Lunch was a delicious combination of chicken, roast veggies, quinoa salad, and Pelligrino with local wine. Probably the healthiest lunch I had all week. Evergreen goes above and beyond when it comes to providing lunch. No brown bag lunches here! This company is quite familiar to me. Real plates and utensils!? Who doesn't enjoy a little luxury in the forest?

# Discovering the San Juan Islands

If you're planning your first trip to the San Juan Islands, check out the helpful tips below! The shorter your stay in the Islands, the more critical it is to plan. Booking boat reservations, hotels, activities, and meals in advance will make your trip go more smoothly. This is your guide to your first island getaway! Also, remember to set your thoughts to island time and join us in enjoying and safeguarding the islands we cherish.

### What are the San Juan Islands?

There are 172 designated islands and reefs in San Juan County, but the four ferry-served islands, San Juan Island (with the county seat Friday Harbor), Orcas Island, Lopez Island, and Shaw Island, are the most populous and provide the great bulk of housing, dining, and tourism opportunities.

### How can I go to the San Juan Islands?

Whether you take a Washington State Ferry from Anacortes, fly from Seattle, or SeaTac Intl. Airport on a Kenmore Air seaplane, wheeled plane, or regional flight, rent a car or take an airporter shuttle from SeaTac, or board the seasonal San Juan Clipper from Seattle's waterfront, arriving at the ferry terminal or boarding your plane marks the start of your San Juan Island vacation.

Coming up for only one day? Consider leaving your car behind and walking to the Washington State Ferry, renting a water taxi, or flying by charter plane. No matter where you're coming from, there are innovative transportation options to make the most of your day trip.

### Getting Here
Make ferry reservations or book a seaplane flight from Seattle to San Juan Island.
By Airplane

### Winter Events and Specials
Celebrate the calm season with a winter retreat! Discover hotel offers and experiences for a healthy weekend or romantic break to the Islands.

### Start planning.

## What shall I do?

Here's a great dilemma: what will you do first on your trip to the San Juan Islands? Go whale-watching? Go kayaking, cycling around Lopez, or climbing Mount Constitution on Orcas Island? Every island provides a multitude of options; fortunately, you can't go wrong.

**Where should we stay?**

Each island has its distinct environment, eating, and entertainment options, but all promise high-quality lodgings. Private cabins overlooking the water, hotels in the heart of town, and cozy B&Bs tucked away in pastoral beauty; are everything here, allowing you a variety of atmospheres and possibilities to enjoy your island vacation. Our accommodation listings will get you one step closer to your vacation.

The San Juan Islands Pledge is straightforward: by acting as an environmentally and socially responsible guest, you are actively contributing to the future of the San Juan Islands.

**Getting to the San Juan islands**

There are numerous routes to get to the San Juan Islands, and each one offers a unique and breathtaking adventure. The shorter your stay on the islands, the more crucial it is to plan. Booking activities, transportation, housing, and meals in advance will help your trip go smoothly and increase your chances of getting your top pick!

If you're traveling from out of state, fly into SEA (Seattle-Tacoma) or Bellingham airports in Washington, or Vancouver, B.C. airport in Canada. From there, you can drive or take a bus to Anacortes, WA, where you can board a Washington

State Ferry to the San Juan Islands. You can also get to the islands by boarding a small plane or seaplane from Seattle, Everett, Bellingham, and other cities, or by private boat.

**Out-of-Service Routes: The** Washington State Ferry route to and from Sidney, British Columbia from Friday Harbor and Anacortes is currently discontinued until further notice. The San Juan Clipper direct from Seattle to Friday Harbor is also unavailable in 2024.

The Puget Sound Express passenger ferry sails from Port Townsend to Friday Harbor seasonally.

Getting Around The Islands

There is a lot to do once you get to the Islands! Discover the history, arts, and culture that make the San Juans unique by biking, boating, driving, taking a bus, trolley, or moped. Follow the Scenic Byway for the entire island experience. The Scenic Byway is divided into three sections: 30 miles along the stunning blue marine highway (Washington State Ferries routes), a driving tour around San Juan Island, and a driving tour of Orcas Island. To get from one island to another, take the inter-island ferry. Have fun on your adventure!

# Chapter 4: Cultural Experiences and Artistic Venues

You can visit as many museums as you want during your stay, and the discount is valid for up to four persons staying in the hotel room, making it ideal for group excursions with friends or family. You can locate the whole list of museums at seattlemuseummonth.com, but how do you choose? Let's get started, and I'll make some suggestions based on your interests.

Since 1933, the Seattle Art Museum (SAM) has served as the Pacific Northwest's headquarters for world-class visual arts. In the center of downtown Seattle, light-filled galleries encourage you to explore permanent collections and special exhibitions. SAM's extensive collection includes Asian, African, Islamic, European, Oceanic, modern, and contemporary art, as well as decorative arts and design. Visitors particularly like the stunning Native American galleries and the charming Porcelain Room. Calder: In Motion, an exhibition by the legendary American artist who revolutionized sculpture, will be on view in

February, with more than 45 works being presented publicly for the first time.

The newly restored Seattle Asian Art Museum is not to be missed. Housed in a stunning art deco edifice in Volunteer Park, the expanded Asian Art Museum defies convention by offering a thematic, rather than geographic or chronological, survey of art from the world's largest continent. Highlights of February include international artist Anida Yoeu Ali's solo exhibition.

Olympic Sculpture Park is SAM's free outdoor art venue. In the summer, it is crowded with dog walkers, runners, and strollers (both types), but in the winter, you may enjoy the art in peace. The collection contains huge pieces by Richard Serra, Roxy Paine, Jaume Plensa, Louise Bourgeois, and Alexander Calder. While the weather may be cold in February, you may be able to enjoy some stunning clear views of Elliott Bay and the snow-capped Olympic Mountains.

The artist titled the sculpture Echo because "it's such a noisy time that we don't know anymore if our words are coming from us or others." His Echo delivers his message: "Let's try to say our own words."

In Greek mythology, Echo was a mountain nymph. Zeus enjoyed consorting with lovely nymphs and paid them frequent visits on Earth. Hera, Zeus' wife, became suspicious and traveled from Mount Olympus to catch Zeus with the nymphs. Echo faced Hera's anger for attempting to defend Zeus (as he had told her to do), and Hera limited her ability to speak only the last words given to her. So, when Echo met Narcissus and fell in love with him, she was unable to express her feelings and had to watch him fall in love with himself.

One of Seattle's most popular attractions is also its most artistic. Chihuly Garden and Glass, located in Seattle Center, is a colorful and light-filled showcase of Dale Chihuly's work, one of the world's living glass art masters. It never ceases to amaze with its rooms upon rooms of glass, magnificent suspended sculptures, and vibrant gardens. Winter Brilliance is an original light and music installation that uses cutting-edge video projection technology and will be on display through February.

Chihuly Garden and Museum is my favorite museum in Seattle! I thoroughly enjoyed photographing both the indoor glass sculptures and the outside glass garden.

We have a very famous French proverb that says, "Felling like an elephant in a porcelain store!"

This is exactly how I felt as I went with Miya through the Chihuly Museum's glass sculpture collection.

It was lovely but quite stressful.

Fortunately, there were no breakages.

If you're in Seattle, I recommend seeing this one-of-a-kind museum.

Art fans should also consider a quick drive south to Tacoma. In addition to exciting special exhibitions, one of the highlights of visiting the Museum of Glass is the opportunity to see glass craftsmen at work in the Hot Shop Amphitheatre, which is located inside the 90-foot tall steel cone.

BIMA, the Bainbridge Island Museum of Art, is a 30-minute ferry ride from the downtown Seattle waterfront (tip: get on as a foot passenger for ease and savings) and a short stroll away. Admission is always free, but even without the promise of saving money, this small jewel of a museum is a worthwhile expedition for a fascinating look at the Puget Sound region's art and craft, housed in an amazing LEED Gold building. An onsite café is ideal for a lunch break, or a stroll a little further into town for more delicious options. The boat trip is another famous Northwest experience, with spectacular vistas of the Seattle cityscape and Elliott Bay.

Another hidden gem just east of downtown Seattle is the Frye Art Museum, which is also free. Established in 1952, the museum is today noted for its contemporary art exhibitions that address current themes, as well as thought-provoking programs.

Finally, the Henry Art Gallery, Washington State's oldest art museum, welcomes you to the University of Washington campus. Don't be fooled by its antiquity; the Henry specializes in presenting world-renowned contemporary artists and developing rising talent.

My recommendation: Don't miss Light Reign, the Skyspace by renowned artist James Turrell. This immersive installation is one of my favorite meditative areas in town.

In this Chihuly Garden and Glass review, I'll give a variety of ideas to help you make the most of your visit to this spectacular exhibition. The museum and gardens highlight the remarkable work of Dale Chihuly, a world-renowned glass artist.

From breathtaking chandeliers to elaborate glass sculptures situated in an exquisite landscape, it provides a one-of-a-kind and visually exciting trip into the world of contemporary glass art.

On my recent trip, I asked the tour guide and docents for their advice and finest ideas, which I will share with you. This book will offer you all of the information you need to organize your visit to the Chihuly Garden and Glass.

**Is Chihuly Garden and Glass worth it?** The first question most people ask is, "Is Chihuly Garden and Glass worth it?" Unless you have a tight budget, the answer is yes! It is such a visual joy and one-of-a-kind experience that it is well worth including on your trip to Seattle. That being said, it is very pricey given its size, so I recommend that tourists purchase their tickets as part of a combo pass. Stand-alone tickets cost $26-$35 per person, but if you plan to visit several sites in the area, use the links below to purchase a combo ticket with the Space Needle or a Seattle City Pass, which includes admission to multiple local use performances, playgrounds, gardens, sculptures, an interactive fountain, and multiple cultural and musical events.

**How Long Does it Take to Walk Through Chihuly Garden and Glass?** When planning a trip to Seattle, most people want to know "How long does it take to go through the Chihuly Garden and Glass?" Visitors spend an average of 1.5 to 2 hours viewing the displays and outdoor garden. However, your pace may differ based on the amount of time you have available, your level of interest, and how much of the museum you want to see.

In this Chihuly Garden and Glass review, I recommend setting aside three hours to observe the glass-blowing demonstration and short videos. This also allows you to join a free docent-led tour, eat a snack at the eccentric cafe, and spend some quiet time on the benches throughout the exhibit. If you finish early, you'll have plenty of fascinating things to pick from at Seattle Center.

**Chihuly Museum:** What to Expect. You will start your Chihuly Museum adventure at the entrance where you can purchase tickets in person either at the counter or via kiosks. Again, I recommend buying a combo pass, which can be purchased in advance. There is also a coat check where you may leave your jackets and bulky bags. Umbrella strollers are permitted, but not larger models. There are also wheelchairs accessible to use.

Chihuly Garden & Glass Tour When you enter the museum, look for the hours for the free docent-led tours.

These are fascinating and instructive, and you can obtain answers to all of your exhibition-related inquiries. Every day, various English-language tours are offered.

The Exhibition Hall includes eight very stunning gallery rooms! Dale Chihuly's iconic chandeliers are one of the museum's highlights. However, the museum's collection extends well beyond these chandeliers, with a broad range of sculptures such as the famed glass boats, bowls, and the stunning Mille Fiori garden.

**Exhibition Hall**: Education Station. Also in the Exhibition Hall is the Education Station, which is staffed by a friendly and educated docent and allows you to touch and feel many types of glass and materials used in the glassblowing process. You can also ask questions and receive plenty of helpful tips.

Chihuly Glasshouse and Its Hours You will next proceed to the famed Glasshouse, the museum's centerpiece. This glass and steel structure houses one of Chihuly's greatest suspended sculptures, a spectacular variety of reds, oranges, and yellows. There is lots of sitting, and this is an excellent spot for some quiet observation of the surroundings.

The sculpture also powerfully frames the Space Needle, which soars above it, providing stunning views and photographs. The Glasshouse is occasionally rented out for special parties, and it is not constantly open. Because the Glasshouse hours vary from those of the rest of the museum, check the website for the exact hours on the day you intend to visit.

Chihuly Garden As much as I enjoy the indoor exhibits, the garden is my personal favourite. The design is simply breathtaking. The location of the glass sculptures emphasizes the architecture of the neighboring buildings, such as the Glasshouse and the Space Needle. The juxtaposition of the sculptures with their natural settings, however, brings the experience to life.

The plants complement each of the sculptures, which were carefully selected for their colors, textures, and movement in the wind. The Chihuly Garden is small, but there are several vignettes that you will want to see.

Chihuly Theatre As you leave the garden, make time to see the theater. Several short films on Chihuly and his work will help you have a better understanding and appreciation for what you've seen in the museum.

Chihuly Museum's Gift Shop If you're seeking souvenirs to remember your visit, check by the Chihuly Museum Gift Shop. It is a huge gift shop that sells artwork, apparel, stationery, jewelry, and more. They sell numerous goods using Chihuly artwork, as well as those painstakingly crafted by local PNW artists.

Chihuly Garden & Glass Restaurant Even if you're not hungry, check out The Bar at Chihuly Garden and Glass. It is embellished with over 25 of the artist's collections, which range from tin toys to plastic radios. This results in a weird and distinct dining experience. They feature a large drink selection, much of it is locally sourced, and the cuisine is inspired by the Pacific Northwest.

Chihuly Garden and Glass Photographs This museum encourages photography, and you will most likely want to record most of the experience on camera. Tripods and selfie sticks are not allowed.
To stay present with the artwork, consider fully savoring each area before returning to specific pieces to capture.

You can use your flash indoors and outdoors. The final gallery room, the Macchia Forest, houses a fanciful array of bowls.
He developed the technique of placing an opaque layer of glass inside each bowl.

When I asked one of the docents what she wanted visitors to know about the museum, she was eager to inform me about the effect of lighting on these bowls. She used her phone's flashlight to demonstrate how the colors change greatly depending on the angle of lighting. It was remarkable, and the museum allows visitors to observe with a flashlight.

Chihuly Glass Museum Parking I've located parking near Seattle Center hundreds of times, and my best suggestion is to allow plenty of time to find a spot or utilize public transportation.

There are parking facilities and lots throughout the neighborhood, as well as street and valet parking. Most downtown parking is pricey and is typically paid for using parking apps on your phone.

If you're visiting Seattle from out of town and staying downtown, taking public transportation is the best method to get to the Chihuly Museum. You may travel the monorail which is perhaps the least priced attraction ticket in the city!

**The Best Time to Visit Chihuly Garden and Glass.** The best time to visit Chihuly Garden and Glass is during the week when it is less busy. Crowds are also smaller in the mornings and after 5:00 p.m. Summer weekends are the most congested. The outdoor sculptures are stunning, yet they differ in day and dramatic midnight lighting.

More Glass Art in Washington A short trip south of Seattle will take you to the world-famous Museum of Glass and the neighboring Chihuly Bridge of Glass in Tacoma. If you enjoyed Chihuly Garden and Glass, you'll adore this museum. I hope my Chihuly Glass and Garden Review has helped you plan a wonderful trip! With the information in this book, you can confidently plan your visit and make the most of your time at this stunning Seattle destination. The Chihuly Garden and Glass offers an extraordinary experience, and I hope you have a nice time.

## Pike Place Market

When I initially relocated to the greater Seattle region, I planned to visit Pike Place Market once a week to get fresh flowers for our home. I've lived here for seven years. Do you know how many times I've picked up flowers at Pike Place? Once. For years, Pike Place Market overwhelmed me. It was always congested, and there were so many little places to stop, but I wasn't sure which ones were the nicest, and I felt like I spent half of my time just navigating crowds and going from one end to the other without seeing much of anything.

I made an effort to understand more about the market because it has such a rich history. I believe most tourists understand that Pike Place is iconic to Seattle, but they don't know why or what else they should see. I'll make sure you get the most out of your Pike Place Market visit, and I believe it will make you appreciate it even more. So here's a local's perspective on Pike Place. Take notes, buddies!

If you add a s to your name, locals will immediately recognize that you are not from the area. It's called Pike Place Market, not Pikes Place or Pike Market. You will fit right in whether you name it Pike Place or The Market.

### History of Pike Place Market.
Pike Place debuted in August 1907. It is one of the longest-running public farmer's markets in the United States. The Market looks out over Elliott Bay's coastline on Puget Sound. It is called after the

street it runs on, Pike Street, and is Seattle's most popular tourist site.

When you think of a farmer's market, you generally envision veggies, and in the Pacific Northwest, fish. But Pike Place is more than just that. It has a diverse range of handicrafts, excellent art, and some of the best buskers around! Seattle's local music favorites, such as Brandi Carlise and Dave Matthews, have occasionally been over to perform.

**The Pike Place Market Foundation**

The Pike Place Market Foundation was established in 1982 to assist the core of the market--its people.

Did you know that The Market has a preschool? Because there were no inexpensive childcare services nearby, vendors were forced to bring their newborns and young children to their stalls. A preschool has opened, and families pay for quality care on a sliding basis.

Did you know that over 500 people are living in eight separate structures across the market? There is an assisted living facility and low-income housing. A senior center offers a warm and comfortable environment as well as a place to eat a hot meal, and a community health care center helps to eliminate health disparities in and around the market area.

There's even a secret Pike Place Market garden staffed by volunteers who grow veggies for the local food bank.

Many of these programs are funded by donations to Rachel and Billie, the Market piggybanks.

So, when you see them, give them some money because some fantastic things are going on thanks to donors who come to the market.

**best time if you want to visit Pike Place Market.**

Every day, traders at Pike Place Market disassemble and reassemble their stands. After closing at about 6 PM, the market remains calm until around 10 AM. I love visiting there in the morning.. I enjoy watching the vendors set up. I enjoy strolling the halls, watching the food being prepared, and enjoying the aromas of all the freshly baked goods.

I also believe it is the finest time to visit the original Starbucks, which is located at 1912 Pike Place. The line at Starbucks can get long, and it's not uncommon to wait an hour or more for a drink or a specialty mug or tumbler that you can't get anywhere else, but if you arrive early and stop by before The Market opens, you might be able to walk right in and enjoy your favorite drink while sipping and watching the magic of the market as it opens for the day.

Another place that opens early is Le Panier. This real French bakery opens at 7 a.m. and uses traditional techniques to create some of the best French specialties on the West Coast.

Shop Like a Local at Pike Place.

Locals rarely wait in line for coffee at Starbucks. My favorite is Storyville. Storyville is tucked away up a few flights of stairs, but you can find it by looking for their sign out front, just beyond the flower shop and towards the renowned Pike Place Market sign.

The view from Storyville is one of my favorites, so take a seat at the window and people-watch. You might be lucky. The staff frequently goes about, offering portions of free cake at odd intervals throughout the day.

Matt's in the Market is located right next door. I usually recommend this tiny location for lunch. Arrive when it opens and request to sit by the window.

I spent my adult life thinking I didn't enjoy yogurt until I tried Ellenos. Oh.my.word. It's like soft-serve ice cream, but better. An American flight attendant was flying to Australia when she met a Greek father-son pair that made small-batch Greek yogurt. Every visit, I get a walk-about-cup {typically Marionberry} and meander around the market.

There are plenty of fresh flavors prepared with locally sourced products.

You can't go to the market without stopping at Daily Dozen Donuts for a dozen nice, toasty cinnamon sugar donuts. After getting your donuts {or before}, walk down the steps to the gum wall.

When you're done with the gum wall, return upstairs and see if you can find the hidden garden. It's hidden, but with a little off-the-beaten-path exploration, you can find it. You might be rewarded with a stunning view of the city.

If the fishmongers are throwing, stand back by Rachel the Pig and witness the magic. This area can get crowded, but it's entertaining to watch these guys do their jobs. Pike Place Fish Market also ships, so place your order for fresh fish!

Rachel's Ginger Beer is one of my new favorites. I bring my growler to have it refilled, and I also receive a cup of Blood Orange to drink.

Visit Beecher's and observe the cheesemaking process through the glass. I like to grab a tiny container of cheese curds and couple it with a baguette from Le Panier (if you stopped earlier). Visit DeLaurenti for more picnic items {try the cone}, then relax at Victor Steinbrueck Park and watch the ferries pass past.

If you need a little dessert, the Made in Washington Store on Post Alley sells Seattle Chocolate, which is excellent! Try the Champagne flavor; it has candy pop rocks and is a nice little treat.

After a quick picnic, head down to the retail establishments. There are many market vendors upstairs, but they are frequently too busy for me to enjoy, so I prefer to escape the crowds and spend some time off the usual road.

Marnin Saylor is the first new shop to open downstairs in over 25 years! They spent six years as a craft seller, setting up and ripping down every day, before settling on what I believe is the best site in the market. The pink window provides the ideal backdrop for the Great Wheel.

Marnin Saylor has locations around the market. You wouldn't know it for its plush cat donuts, but the business tells a tale and provides a genuine experience. Don't be afraid to explore back alleys, downstairs halls, and off-the-beaten route to see what you'll come upon. Every visit, I discover a new favorite spot or hidden gem.

# Chapter 5: Food and Drink: The Culinary Scene

Washington State's culinary scene is rich and diversified, reflecting its geographical variety and cultural influences. Here's a list of some of the must-see food and drink experiences in Washington:

## Seattle's Coffee Culture

- **Location:** Seattle is recognized as the coffee capital of the USA.
- **Highlights:** Home to Starbucks' original location in Pike Place Market. Numerous artisanal coffee establishments, like Espresso Vivace, Stumptown Coffee Roasters, and Seattle Coffee Works, provide unique mixes and brewing methods.
- **Must Try:** Aside from traditional espresso, enjoy local delicacies like the 'Seattle Latte', which features unique flavor infusions.

# Wine Tasting in Yakima Valley

- **Location:** Central Washington, approximately 2 hours from Seattle.
- **Highlights:** Yakima Valley, part of the wider Columbia Valley AVA, is well-known for its wineries and vineyards. Visit Owen Roe, Hedges Family Estate, and Red Willow Vineyard.
- **Must Try:** Known for its Merlot, Cabernet Sauvignon, and Chardonnay. Don't miss the Rieslings and Syrahs, which are gaining popularity.

## Pacific Northwest Seafood.

- **Location:** The coastal sections of Washington, including Seattle's Pike Place Market and waterfront restaurants.
- **Highlights:** Fresh seafood like salmon, Dungeness crab, oysters, and clams. Famous restaurants include the Walrus and Carpenter and Elliott's Oyster House.
- **Must-Try:** salmon prepared in a variety of ways, fresh oysters, and clam chowder.

# Local Farmers' Markets

It can be found throughout Washington, including Seattle (Pike Place Market), Tacoma, Olympia, and Spokane.

- **Highlights:** These markets sell local produce, artisanal products, and street cuisine, and provide an insight into local culture.

- **Must-Try:** Seasonal fruits such as apples and cherries, locally made cheeses, and handcrafted products. Don't miss out on the street food sellers who provide a variety of local and international cuisines.

## Additional Recommendations:

- **Apple Products in Wenatchee:** Wenatchee, known as the apple capital, offers fresh apple cider and pies.

- **Craft Beer in Spokane and Seattle:** With a thriving craft beer culture, these cities have a diverse selection of local brews.

- **Raspberry Desserts in Lynden:** The area is famous for its raspberry fields.

## Drinks to Try:

- **Craft Beers:** A diverse selection of locally brewed beers, IPAs, and stouts.

- **Local Wines:** Discover the state's numerous wine areas beyond Yakima Valley, such as Walla Walla and the Puget Sound AVA.
- **Cider:** Washington is one of the top apple producers, resulting in a thriving cider-making sector.

**Must-Try Foods:**
- **Cedar-Planked Salmon:** A popular local cooking method for salmon.
- **Geoduck:** A type of clam commonly eaten as sushi or sashimi.
- **Marionberry Pie:** Delicious pies made using a regional berry variety.
- **Teriyaki:** Inspired by Seattle's Asian American community, this has become a local fast-food favorite.

Each of these experiences not only gives you a taste of Washington's gastronomic delights but also a glimpse into the state's culture and history. For guests, it's an opportunity to discover and appreciate the diverse local food and beverage scene.

# Chapter 6: Festivals and Events

## Seattle International Film Festival

The Seattle International Film Festival (SIFF) is an annual film festival held in Seattle, Washington, United States, since 1976. It usually occurs in late May and/or early June. It is one of the world's major film festivals, with a wide lineup of mostly independent and foreign films, as well as a strong number of documentaries.

SIFF 2006 included over 300 films and 160,000 visitors; also, it was the first SIFF to incorporate a location in neighboring Bellevue, Washington, following an unsuccessful early attempt. However, in 2008, the festival returned to Seattle and had a slightly lower number of feature films. Over 400 films were played during the 2010 festival, which took place mostly in downtown Seattle and its surrounding districts, as well as Renton, Kirkland, and Juanita Beach Park.

## History

The festival began in 1976 at the Moore Egyptian Theater, a then-independent cinema, under the management of Jim Duncan, Dan Ireland, and Darryl Macdonald.

The first SIFF featured Glenda Jackson's "Hedda," Louis Malle's "Black Moon," and Luis Buñuel's "Phantom of Liberty." "The Rocky Horror Picture Show was the unnamed secret "sneak preview." Rajeev Gupta directed the inaugural Third Festival in 1978.

It doubled the number of films and increased attendance by 50% compared to the second festival.

The first five festivals took place at the Moore Egyptian.

The Moore Theatre is now known by its original name and serves as a concert venue. When the Moore Egyptian's owners, Dan Ireland and Darryl Macdonald, lost their lease, they established the Egyptian Theater in a disused Masonic Temple on Seattle's Capitol Hill. The Egyptian theater is still a popular festival location today, though the festival now normally uses approximately a half-dozen cinemas (including its own SIFF Cinema in Seattle Center, which has been in operation since 2007), with the exact roster varying from year to year.

During the 1980s, SIFF viewers gained a reputation for enjoying films that did not fit into traditional industry niches, such as Richard Rush's multilayered The Stunt Man (1980).[Citation needed] SIFF was essential in bringing Dutch films to the United States market, notably filmmaker Paul Verhoeven's first major American premiere.

**The character of the festival**
The festival features the four-film "Secret Festival". Those who attend the Secret Festival have no idea what they will witness, and they must swear a pledge not to mention what they have seen later.
In general, SIFF is known as an "audience festival" rather than an "industry festival".The festival frequently coincides with the Cannes Film Festival, which might reduce participation by industry executives; in 2007, there were two days of overlap on May 24 and 25.

The SIFF group also curates the Global Lens film series, the Screenwriters Salon, and Futurewave (K-12 programming and youth engagement); manages SIFF-A-Go-Go travel programs (arranged trips to various cinema festivals), and co-curates the 1 Reel Film Festival at Bumbershoot and the Sci-Fi Shorts Film Festival at the Science Fiction Museum and Hall of Fame.

Longhouse Media launched the SuperFly Filmmaking Experience in 2006, in collaboration with the Seattle International Film Festival, to bring youth from various backgrounds together to work collaboratively on film projects that promote awareness of indigenous issues and mutual understanding of cultures. Fifty teenagers from throughout the United States arrive in Seattle before traveling to a nearby Pacific Northwest reserve to create four films in 36 hours.

# *Washington State Apple Blossom Festival*

Blossoms, brews, bikes, and more flocked to the Wenatchee Valley from April 27 to May 7. In 2023, Washington's oldest major celebration celebrated its 104th year. Sue Wagner, a New Zealand transplant in Wenatchee, is the driving force behind the Apple Blossom Festival. Wagner arranged the first Apple Blossom Festival in May 1920, recognizing Wenatchee as a significant apple-growing location as well as women's contributions to America's growth.

Over the last century, visitors from all over the world have come to enjoy this family-friendly community celebration of Wenatchee Valley's people, traditions, and fruit business.

**Here are some of the festival's events:**

Blossoms and Brews Beer Garden (April 27–May 7): The Blossoms & Brews Beer Garden, located inside Memorial Park near the Entertainment Stage, sells local beer, wine, seltzers, and ciders during the event. It's a terrific opportunity to sample a range of Central Washington-made beverages.

Memorial Park Food Fair, April 27–May 7: The Food Fair takes place throughout the festival. More than 20 booths serve delicious funnel cakes, substantial BBQs, numerous ethnic cuisines, crepes, ice cream, espresso, caramel apples, elephant ears, pizza, sandwiches, and more.

GESA Credit Union Entertainment Stage, April 27-May 7: Local and national bands will perform classic rock, country, big band jazz, reggae, and other genres throughout lunch and dinner on weekdays and all day on weekends.

**Funtastic Shows Carnival, April 28-May 7:** Funtastic Shows is America's seventh largest carnival, including roughly 25 rides and games for all ages, as well as plenty of food. The carnival is held at the Wenatchee Valley Mall in East

Wenatchee, at the Sportsman's Warehouse parking lot at 611 Valley Mall Parkway.

**Apple Blossom Musical, May 3-13:** The Numerica Performing Arts Center and Music Theater of Wenatchee present the Broadway mega sensation Shrek The Musical. Tickets are on sale at the Numerica Performing Arts Center and online at numericapac.org.

**Classy Chassis Parade & Car Show, May 5-6:** The Classy Chassis Parade begins at 6 p.m. on May 5 and will feature new cars, antique vehicles, and more. A live band will perform at Gateway Park from 8 to 10 p.m. following the parade. The car show occurs on May 6 and will provide an up-close look at some of the "Classy Chassis".

**Arts & Crafts Fair, May 5-7:** This three-day festival in Memorial Park will feature 140 vendors selling handcrafted things such as clothes, music, wood, ceramics, candles/soap, metal, country, jewelry, leather, and more.

The Wenatchee Valley Velo Club organizes the Tour de Bloom, a three-day, four-race cycling event from May 5-7. The Waterville Road Race will take place on Friday, followed by the Palisades Merckx-style Time Trial and the Downtown Wenatchee Criterium on Saturday, and the Plain Road Race featuring a hilltop finish on Sunday.

**Stemilt Grand Parade, May 6:** The cannon goes off at 11 a.m. to herald the Washington State Apple Blossom Festival Grand Parade, which has been continuing strong since the festival's inception in 1919. The procession attracts around 100,000 spectators each year. The parade lineup, which begins with the classic Apple Blossom Fun Run and the daring maneuvers of the Seattle Police Motorcycle Drill Team, features bands from all across the Northwest, as well as colorful floats and horse units.

The festival also features the Art 4 Kidz contest, the Youth Day celebration and parade, the Stand Against Racism: Until Justice Just Is march and other events.

# Bumbershoot Music & Arts Festival

Bumbershoot embodies the essence of Seattle's Labor Day weekend. The event made a triumphant return in 2023. Bumbershoot is Seattle's largest music and arts event, held over a three-day holiday weekend at Seattle Center. It's one of the must-see events of the year in Seattle.

With over 100 performers performing on six distinct stages, the music at Bumbershoot is our favorite part. Bumbershoot boasts the "most diverse and carefully curated musical lineups in the world." Bumbershoot genuinely has something for everyone, from Grammy Award winners to old-time rockers to emerging hip-hop performers. All weekend long, music can be heard bursting around Seattle Center. Tove and I were only there for one day last year, but we got to see almost ten different bands. While the event attracts national and international performances, it takes pride in promoting local performers.

While music is the most popular event at Bumbershoot, comedy attracts thousands of people to Seattle over Labor Day weekend. Almost 30 different comic artists will perform on three distinct stages throughout the weekend. Bumbershoot, like the music, features well-known national and local comedians to entertain us. There's stand-up comedy, improv, and even live podcasting. The comedy festival at Bumbershoot is a must-see. It's a common topic of talk among the crowd.

In addition to music and comedy, Bumbershoot hosts a film festival, literary arts and lecture series, a theater stage, and visual art exhibits and spectacles.

Fashion, popular independent films, local shows, and much more will be on exhibit over the three-day weekend at Seattle Center. Bumbershoot is genuinely a music and arts festival, and it is regarded as one of the largest in the country.

Although there is a lot of cannabis smoking in the crowd and occasional harsh language on stage, Bumbershoot is a family-friendly event. Children under the age of ten are admitted for free with a paying adult, and there is even an area of the festival dedicated to children called "Youngershoot". When Tove and I passed by, we noticed art project stations, miniature foot-powered cars with a small village to drive around, and other activities.

To access Bumbershoot, you must purchase tickets; however, once inside, everything is free (save for food and merchandise). To see a comedy act, you'll need an additional ticket (which you can acquire at a booth once you enter the festival; tickets are limited to one per person per day), but they're free. You do not need an additional ticket to watch the main stage, but you must wait in line. That means you have to get in line early or risk not getting in. It may sound like a chore, but it's not that horrible. Even though the line stretched over the festival grounds, Tove and I only had to wait 40 minutes to witness the act.

Every year, hundreds of other festivals take place in Seattle, but Bumbershoot is by far our favorite.

We could honestly spend the entire Labor Day weekend enjoying the activities. There's nothing better than roaming around and falling in love with a band you had never heard of before. That always happens to us at Bumbershoot. It's Seattle's ultimate festival. Do not miss out on the fun!

# Skagit Valley Tulip Festival

**Top Things to Do during the 2024 Skagit Valley Tulip Festival**

The Skagit Valley Tulip Festival, one of Western Washington's most anticipated springtime events, returns in April. The driving tour allows tourists to explore the many fields between La Conner and Mount Vernon, with stops at scheduled events and favored gardens.

Tulip Town and RoozenGaarde will have tulip displays in their separate gardens where visitors may view the blossoms and take photographs.

Although the tulip fields are the major draw, touring the region's lovely villages, fun cafes, and breathtaking natural scenery is also a lot of fun. Don't miss out on the biggest attractions and activities at this year's event.

**Tips for enjoying the Tulip Festival**

**1:** Both Tulip Town and RoozenGaarde offer free parking, but admission is charged. Purchase your ticket in advance.

2: Along with the exhibits at RoozenGaarde and Tulip Town, there are other fields of "free range" tulips. Their location changes year to year due to crop rotations. Look for highway signage indicating the "Tulip Route." You can view the fields and take photos from the roadside, but never enter an open tulip field. If you can't locate a spot to pull over, there will be free parking near select fields.

**3:** Visit the event on a weekday when there are fewer attendees. Do not forget your boots. April is generally rainy, resulting in muddy fields.

**4**: Because the main Mount Vernon exit (Exit 226) frequently backs up in April, consider taking Highway 20 to Exit 230 instead.

5: Although the festival officially runs throughout April, nature determines peak bloom time, so check the official bloom status to stay up to date.

6: Wine tastings and art displays are among the events hosted by local organizations in Mount Vernon, Burlington, La Conner, Conway, Anacortes, Sedro-Woolley, and other nearby areas.

If you arrive during a busy period, expect to wait outdoors or in your car.

**7:** Safety first. In the interest of safety and civility to other festival attendees, do not pull over or park in prohibited areas—and, because these are working farms, do not stroll into the fields.

**8:** Do you want to experience the festival differently? Check out the various tour options available at the event, such as photography excursions, helicopters, vineyards, ice cream tours, and much more.

**Not-to-Miss nearby attractions and events.**

Make your Skagit Valley Tulip Festival visit an enjoyable day of exploring. Here are our suggestions for making the most of your stay, including great family-friendly activities and exploring restaurants, local towns, trails, and more.

The beautiful Kukutali Preserve, located on two connected islands, is a spectacular setting with 2 miles of paths through Douglas fir and madrone forest, driftwood-strewn beaches, and stunning ocean views, including a glimpse of the Deception Pass Bridge.

Because it is jointly owned by Washington State Parks and the Swinomish tribe, it is considered sacred territory and should be treated with greater respect. There are no pets or alcohol allowed, and parking requires a Discover Pass.

The Skagit Valley Tulip Festival combines with another spectacular show of nature. Approximately 35,000 snow geese overwinter in the area, usually until mid-April or early May. The Skagit Wildlife Area's Fir Island Farms Reserve Unit, along Fir Island Road, is the greatest site to see these magnificent creatures.

**Explore La Conner.**

La Conner, one of the Northwest's most appealing small towns, boasts historic buildings filled with local stores and cafés along the Swinomish Channel.

La Conner Brewing Co.'s pub menu features grass-fed beef burgers, enchiladas, pizzas, and other options, as well as housemade beer.

Sustainable seafood shines at The Oyster & Thistle, where French-inspired meals are prepared with meticulous attention to detail in a charming hillside building.

The free Museum of Northwest Art hosts exhibits of very high-quality contemporary art that reflect the cultural richness of the Northwest, including British Columbia and Alaska.

The Butterfly Gardens, which are maintained by the Civic Garden Club, is a calm area where visitors may enjoy views of the town and part of the channel. If the venue is being booked for an event, you may be unable to access it.

The Pacific Northwest Quilt and Fiber Arts Museum, housed in the historic Gaches Mansion, exhibits textile work from around the Pacific Rim and beyond. The exhibitions contain both classic and contemporary pieces.

# Chapter 7: Outdoor Recreation and Sports

The Tri-Cities offers a variety of outdoor activities, including three rivers for paddling, fishing, and floating, as well as miles of trails for bicycling, hiking, and walking.

From biking to bird viewing, the Tri-Cities (Kennewick, Pasco, Richland, and West Richland) are the ideal locations to enjoy most of Washington's outdoors! With little rain and plenty of sunshine, the desert region boasts animal reserves, parks, trails, and green spaces all within city boundaries.

While you are planning and fantasizing about packing, we have several suggested itineraries for you to consider.

Enjoy a bird-watching tour while strolling through the Chamna Natural Preserve; kayak to nearby Bateman Island; hike Badger Mountain or the new Candy Mountain trail to take in the vast, photogenic views of wildflowers; watch a movie under the stars or attend one of the outdoor concerts offered throughout the summer; or grab the kids and some fishing gear and head over to the Family Fishing Pond.

The Tri-Cities are located at the junction of the Columbia, Snake, and Yakima rivers, creating a town with a range of water sports. The Tri-Cities has something for everyone, whether you want to relax with Stand Up Paddle Board (SUP) Yoga or embark on an action-packed jet ski trip. Explore the different alternatives for outdoor recreation in Washington below. Whether you enjoy bike rides, paddling outings, or wildlife observation tours, there is an outdoor experience for you!

# Wildlife

The variety of animals in the Tri-Cities area allows students excellent observation and learning opportunities. Watch the migration of ducks in the fall and spring, and notice the subtle changes in local flora and animals as the weather changes. These fantastic natural places allow you to get up close and personal with Washington State's animals.

There are eight National Wildlife Refuges and Reserves in the Tri-Cities region.

**Amon Creek Nature Preserve**

Amon Basin was formed by the discharge of Amon Creek. Amon Creek and its surrounding wetlands and riparian regions provide a cool haven for species such as beavers, river otters, jackrabbits, and deer. Those who like bird watching can find over 150 species on this refuge.

**Audubon Nature Trail**

The Audubon Nature Trail, located along the Columbia River in Columbia Park, offers a leisurely, paved circle ideal for birdwatchers seeking an easy hike. The route contains a natural pond where you may identify insects and fish. Visitors have noticed deer tracks and other animals.

**Badger Mountain Centennial Preserve**

Badger Mountain Centennial Preserve is one of the last surviving shrub-steppe ecosystems on Tri-Cities' southwestern fringe. Hike, mountain bike, or ride a horse up Badger Mountain for breathtaking views of the Tri-Cities, Columbia, Yakima, and Snake River basins. There is also a diverse population of tiny animals.

Birdwatching aficionados may enjoy the warm climate all year.

Each visit will reveal fresh and distinct species because the region draws both migratory and resident avifauna.

## Bateman Island

Bateman Island is situated on the Columbia River in southern Richland. This amazing island is designated as an Urban Watchable Wildlife Area. The public island is accessible by a tiny land bridge, and some paths allow you to trek or mountain bike around the entire island.

## McNary National Wildlife Refuge

McNary National Wildlife Refuge is an important rest and feeding location for migratory ducks. Depending on the season, visitors can see a variety of animals, songbirds, ducks, and migrating birds. More than 212 bird species are often spotted at the Refuge, including some endangered species.

## Chamna Natural Preserve.

Tapteal Greenway/Chamna Natural Preserve is a 30-mile corridor along the Yakima River that includes trails, informative kiosks, signs, and trail maps. The Yakima River offers an intimate backdrop, passing past farmlands and densely wooded riparian regions.

Kayakers may explore several sloughs, islands, and rapids on a river that is a famous nesting ground for birds and home to a variety of Washington state animals.

Visitors are challenged not by the birding itself, but by finding enough free time to visit all of the various observation spots. Birding in the Tri-Cities is a well-kept secret, and visitors are often blown away by the range of species and abundance of birds.

# Chapter 8: 12 Unique Places to Stay in Washington State in 2024

Are you looking for interesting hotels in Washington State? Look no further! I traveled over this breathtaking region to bring you a curated list of the most outstanding lodgings. From sleeping high on the treetops in lovely treehouses to relaxing on legendary houseboats, every location in this tour is a hidden gem.

In this book, we look at 12 of the greatest hotels and lodgings in Washington. These are not conventional hotels. They are destinations in their own right, each adding a distinctive twist to your travel experience. If you're looking for a lavish retreat, a unique adventure, or a peaceful break, these destinations will take your Washington State experience to new heights. So let's embark on this excursion and discover the beauty and originality of Washington State's lodgings!

The most interesting locations to stay in Washington State right now.

Are you ready to discover the most unusual lodging options in Washington State? This diversified region is well-known for its unique accommodations, which combine natural beauty with particular charm. From quirky historic hotels to quiet nature getaways, Washington State has a variety of alternatives for every sort of tourist. Whether you're looking for adventure, leisure, or a combination of the two, you'll find the right setting. Are you excited to find your ideal Washington getaway? Here are the top unique stays in Washington State that will make your trip genuinely unforgettable!

## 1. Anderson School Hotel

Ever wanted to go back to school simply for the enjoyable parts? That is precisely what you can expect at the Anderson School Hotel in Bothell! This is not your typical Washington State accommodation. It's a 1930s school that has been transformed into an amazing place to stay. Imagine relaxing with a craft drink in an area where lockers and chalkboards are expected.

The coolest part? There is no requirement for a hall pass to explore this area. You may have a drink in the Principal's Office, play pinball in the Woodshop, or skip gym class for a long swim in the pool.

When hunger hits, Tavern on the Square serves far superior food than any school cafeteria I've ever seen.

Discover the Anderson School Hotel, a one-of-a-kind Washington State accommodation that has been renovated from a 1930s school into a treasure. You're only a short drive from Seattle, and the Sammamish River Trail is close by for those who want a lovely bike ride or walk. In addition, the hotel's courtyard is a green refuge ideal for relaxing by the fireplace.

What makes the Anderson School Hotel stand out? It's a combination of eccentric heritage and modern comfort, not to mention local art that conveys stories from the past. It's one of the most enjoyable locations to stay in Washington State, with each corner telling a tale and making your stay part of history.

## 2. Treehouse Point
If you've ever wanted to wake up in the treetops, TreeHouse Point is your fantasy come true. This resort, located just a 30-minute drive east of Seattle and nestled in a verdant forest, is like walking into a fairy tale. You're surrounded by the calm of the Pacific Northwest while yet enjoying all of the amenities of home.

TreeHouse Point is more than just one treehouse; it is an entire hamlet in the canopy! With seven distinct treehouses to select from, each one is a work of rustic beauty and warm atmosphere. These treehouses are heated and provide all of the comforts, such as bedding, towels, and even bathroom supplies. It's the camping experience you've always wanted, without the trouble.

TreeHouse Point provides a magnificent treetop stay—a one-of-a-kind hotel experience in Washington State.
TreeHouse Point provides a wonderful treetop stay that is unlike any other accommodation experience in Washington State. It's not all about staying in your gorgeous treehouse, however. There is a central Lodge for socializing, and if you're planning an event or a celebration, they provide a room for that as well.
Additionally, the cedar-lined bathhouses provide a touch of luxury to your woodland escape.

The combination of excitement and comfort makes TreeHouse Point one of the top locations to stay in Washington State. This location is ideal for nature lovers, romantics, and those looking for a one-of-a-kind vacation. It's an experience that links you to nature while delivering a comfortable and pleasant stay. Trust me when I say that waking up to the sound of the forest will be unforgettable.

### 3. Elks Temple Hotel

The Elks Temple Hotel in Tacoma is the next on our list of the coolest places to stay in Washington. This location is a 1916 Elks Temple that has been transformed into an enormous entertainment destination. Each of its seven stories is a fresh journey, full of excitement and history.

Begin on the ground level with McMenamins Brewery and The Old Hangout, a pub that feels like a journey across the world. It's ideal for a relaxing evening or a fun start to the night. Then there's the Spanish Ballroom, which has live music and an unforgettable atmosphere. It's a must-see for music fans and everyone who likes to have fun.

Discover the Elks Temple Hotel in Tacoma, a 1916 Elks Temple that has been turned into an entertainment destination.

Discover the Elks Temple Hotel in Tacoma, a 1916 Elks Temple that has been turned into an entertainment destination. As you go, each floor offers something fresh. Doc's, located on the third level, is a gaming bar with a view of the ballroom, perfect for a fun night. Also, don't miss the McMenamins Pub on the fourth level; the cuisine is delicious, and the views of Puget Sound's

Commencement Bay are spectacular. It's the ideal location to unwind and take in the view.

But what's the true secret? The illusive Fifth Floor. It's like a secret level in a game, waiting for you to find it. When you get to the guest suites on the sixth and seventh floors, you'll be treated to an overhead light show and an eye-level view of the beautiful internal atrium.

The Elks Temple Hotel is one of those hipster hotels in Washington State that provides more than simply a bed. It's a voyage through history with a humorous twist at each turn. If you're looking for history, entertainment, or simply a nice place to stay, this hotel offers it all!

## 4. Sleepless aboard the Seattle Houseboat

Consider waking up on the water in Seattle, surrounded by the gentle swing of the lake. That is what the Sleepless in Seattle Houseboat offers, a one-of-a-kind experience in Washington State. This houseboat, featured on Discovery Channel's "Ultimate Homes," isn't your normal one. It's a designer fantasy floating on the ocean.

This houseboat is all about luxury and excitement. It has three bedrooms and two bathrooms and covers 1000 square feet, making it ideal for a family or a group of friends. The decks are fantastic; and ideal for morning coffees or nighttime relaxation. There is also moorage accessible for those who own boats. Furthermore, the hot tub contributes to the whole relaxing experience.

Sleepless in Seattle Houseboat is a one-of-a-kind Washington State stay that floats beautifully on the water. Depending on your mood, the dining room may also function as a dance floor or a yoga studio. **What about the kitchen?** It's a chef's dream, with stainless steel countertops and a cool coral aquarium above the sink. It's ideal for preparing a dinner or simply hanging around.

The catch is that there is a minimum stay of 30 days. However, once you're here, you won't want to go. It's great for watersports enthusiasts. Bring your paddleboard, kayak, or windsurfing gear and experience the ideal waterfront lifestyle.

Staying on the Sleepless in Seattle Houseboat allows you to fulfill your waterfront fantasies in one of Washington's most unusual lodgings.

### 5. Sleeping Lady Mountain Resort

Sleeping Lady Mountain Resort, nestled in the beautiful splendor of Icicle Creek and the Cascade Mountains, provides a tranquil vacation that mixes rustic elegance with modern amenities. This resort is one of the greatest spa hotels in Washington State for individuals seeking relaxation and a connection to nature.

Sleeping Lady's accommodations are deliberately organized into clusters of individual rooms, each with complimentary Internet access, hot towel racks, and luxury amenities. The hand-hewn log beds, covered with fine sheets, provide a peaceful night's sleep. After a day touring Leavenworth or the great outdoors, wrap yourself in a luxurious robe and relax in your room with a cup of fair trade coffee or tea.

Sleeping Lady Mountain Resort offers guests a peaceful retreat that elegantly blends natural charm with modern amenities.
Sleeping Lady Mountain Resort offers guests a peaceful retreat that elegantly blends natural charm with modern amenities. The resort's cottages are ideal for individuals traveling in groups or looking for a romantic retreat. The Rookery can accommodate up to eight guests, making it perfect for family holidays or group getaways. For couples, the Eyrie cabin, with its whirlpool bath and own porch, provides an intimate and romantic atmosphere.

The freshly restored Library Suite is a large one-bedroom cabin ideal for those seeking a touch of luxury in their wilderness vacation.

Every aspect of Sleeping Lady Mountain Resort adds to a tranquil and relaxing ambiance. Whether you're looking for a relaxing spa treatment or to explore Leavenworth's natural beauty, this resort provides a unique combination of rustic charm and luxury comforts. Believe me, it's a distinctive location for vacationers looking for a spa getaway in Washington.

### 6. Hotel Crocodile

Rock 'n' roll aficionados can rejoice! Hotel Crocodile in Seattle is not your ordinary lodging. It's a perfect blend of music and flair, making it one of the greatest hotels in Seattle for music and cultural fans. This is where the dynamic essence of Seattle's music culture comes to life, in the center of the city.

Each suite at the Hotel Crocodile pays tribute to Seattle's rich musical legacy. You will be surrounded by mementos depicting the city's famed music culture. The ambiance here is vibrant, ideal for individuals who enjoy a good song and a little history.

And the greatest part? You're just steps away from some of Seattle's most famous music venues, including the hotel's famed music club.

Hotel Crocodile in Seattle combines music and flair, making it an excellent choice for music enthusiasts. Hotel Crocodile in Seattle combines music and flair, making it an excellent choice for music enthusiasts. The hotel provides a unique combination of comfort and style. The rooms are not only themed but also outfitted with all of the contemporary conveniences you want for a comfortable stay. Think luxurious beds, fast internet, and excellent service, all wrapped up in cool, music-themed décor.

For foodies, the hotel's dining selections are delightful. From quick snacks to sophisticated dining, there's something for everyone's taste. When you're ready to explore, Seattle's thriving nightlife, retail, and dining scenes are only a short walk away.

Every visit to Hotel Crocodile is like getting a behind-the-scenes look at Seattle music. It's an immersive experience that goes beyond what you'd expect from a hotel stay, providing a unique view of the city's character. Whether you're a die-hard music fan or simply seeking a unique vacation, this boutique hotel in Washington State hits all of the right notes.

## 7. Whistlin Jacks

Whistlin' Jacks, nestled in Washington State's gorgeous surroundings, stands out as a quiet refuge for visitors looking for a natural break. It's well-known for its rustic appeal and tranquil environment, making it one of the top lodgings in Washington State for nature lovers and those seeking quiet.

Whistlin' Jacks welcomes you with the warmth of a rustic lodge, nestled among the natural splendor of woods and rivers. The cottages provide a cozy, homey atmosphere, ideal for cool Washington evenings. Imagine sitting by a roaring fire or sipping a hot drink on the porch, surrounded by the peace of the forest.

Whistlin' Jacks, nestled in the gorgeous surroundings of Washington State, stands out as a quiet refuge.

Whistlin' Jacks, nestled in the gorgeous surroundings of Washington State, stands out as a quiet refuge. The setting is ideal for outdoor explorers. You're smack in the middle of hiking routes, fishing locations, and breathtaking views. Whistlin' Jacks is the ideal base camp for anybody who enjoys hiking, fishing, or taking a stroll in the woods. The adjacent rivers and trails provide countless chances for exploration and connection with nature.

What genuinely distinguishes Whistlin' Jacks is its combination of comfort and easy access to the outdoors. It's a location where you may appreciate the simplicity of cabin life without giving up comfort. The lodge and cottages are well-furnished for a comfortable and hassle-free stay.

Whistlin' Jacks is a getaway where you may calm down and enjoy the splendor of Washington's natural beauties. If you're seeking a calm solo retreat or a memorable family excursion, our tiny hideaway provides a genuine and personal experience in Washington's wilderness.

## 8. Carson Ridge Cabins

Escape to the peaceful world of Carson Ridge Luxury Cabins, nestled in the charming town of Carson, Washington. These cottages, located 30 minutes from downtown Hood River and an hour from Portland, Oregon, provide a peaceful escape. This location is a good choice for anyone looking for log cabins in Washington State.

Set on 9 acres of beautifully designed gardens, the property is bordered by meadows, towering pine trees, and breathtaking vistas of nearby mountain ranges and the Cascade Mountain Range. You may see deer gently walk through the birch forest or spot a pheasant that lives in these cottages.

Carson Ridge Luxury Cabins in Washington State are an amazing retreat spot.

Every cabin at Carson Ridge is a refuge of comfort and elegance. Private lounging places are ideal for taking in the natural splendor, and the secluded hammock garden provides a relaxing retreat. The cabins themselves are nicely equipped, creating a pleasant, private ambiance with all of the contemporary facilities you want for a relaxing stay.

Carson Ridge's environmental dedication sets it apart for eco-conscious tourists.

The resort's eco-friendly measures include a recycling program, energy-saving lighting, and the use of ecologically friendly building materials. They also provide electric vehicle (EV) charging facilities for their visitors.

If you're looking for a romantic getaway or a calm solitary retreat, Carson Ridge Luxury Cabins provides a one-of-a-kind experience that mixes rustic beauty with modern amenities. You may enjoy the peacefulness of nature, the comfort of your cabin, and the knowledge that you are staying in an environmentally friendly location.

## 9. Inn in the Market

The Inn at the Market is a hidden treasure among downtown Seattle hotels, located in the center of the city's busy Pike Place Market. This boutique hotel provides a unique perspective on the city, blending luxury with the colorful energy of Seattle's most famous market.

The Inn at the Market is conveniently located among some of Seattle's most popular attractions. Explore the historic market, enjoy fresh seafood, or take a quick walk to the Seattle Art Museum. The seaside is also close, ideal for individuals who enjoy breathtaking vistas and fresh ocean air.

Discover the Inn at the Market, one of Seattle's best downtown hotels.
The Inn's rooms provide a calm escape from the rush and bustle of the city. With sophisticated design and comfy furniture, they provide a pleasant stay right in the heart of Seattle. Many accommodations have breathtaking views of Puget Sound, giving a unique touch to your vacation.

The Inn at the Market's rooftop terrace distinguishes it as one of Seattle's premier luxury hotels. Guests may enjoy panoramic views of the downtown skyline and Elliott Bay. It's the ideal setting for a sunset cocktail or a peaceful hour to appreciate Seattle's splendor.

The Inn at the Market is a fantastic choice for tourists looking for a trendy, pleasant stay close to many of Seattle's top attractions. It combines the comfort and convenience of a downtown hotel with the charm and personality of a boutique lodging.

## 10. The Edgewater

For individuals looking for a place to stay in Seattle, The Edgewater is a top choice. Located on the city's waterfront, this hotel provides a one-of-a-kind experience that mixes the ambiance of a boutique hotel with stunning views of Elliott Bay and the Olympic Mountains.

The Edgewater's unique waterfront position distinguishes it from other boutique hotels in Seattle. Guests may have the unique experience of staying in a room that spans the bay, providing an unrivaled connection to the sea. The hotel's nautical style, replete with river rock fireplaces and rustic furniture, contributes to its distinct appeal.

The Edgewater is located on the waterfront and combines boutique charm with stunning views.
The Edgewater is located on the waterfront and combines boutique charm with stunning views.

Seattle's lively attractions are only a short walk away from the hotel.

The famed Space Needle, Pike Place Market, and the busy downtown are all easily accessible. After a day of exploration, visitors may return to The Edgewater to unwind and watch the boats pass by from their accommodation.

Dining at The Edgewater is an adventure unto itself. The Six Seven Restaurant serves superb food with amazing sea views. It's the ideal setting for a romantic supper or a memorable occasion.

With its distinctive waterfront location, cozy but opulent environment, and accessibility to Seattle's main attractions, The Edgewater provides an exceptional stay for those looking for something really special in the heart of the city.

## 11. Sagecliffe Resort & Spa

Sagecliffe Resort and Spa, located on the cliffs above the Columbia River, is a peaceful haven and unquestionably one of the top spa resorts in Washington. This resort is ideal for visitors seeking leisure and rejuvenation in the breathtaking natural splendor of Washington State.

The resort's unique setting provides stunning views of the Columbia River and its neighboring vineyards. It's an ideal destination for nature lovers and those looking for a calm escape.

The spa at Sagecliffe is a standout, with a variety of treatments meant to calm and refresh. Guests may enjoy massages, facials, and body treatments while admiring the tranquil surroundings.

Sagecliffe Resort and Spa is a tranquil haven among Washington's premier spa resorts. Outdoor fans will appreciate the resort's closeness to hiking trails and the Gorge Amphitheatre, one of the country's most well-known performance venues.

Sagecliffe is a wonderful setting for a concert, hiking, or just relaxing.

Sagecliffe is a favorite destination for individuals looking for a soothing and revitalizing spa getaway in Washington State.

## 12. Snug Harbor Resort

For those looking for a calm vacation in the San Juan Islands, Snug Harbor Resort on Mitchell Bay is a hidden gem. This resort has waterfront rooms that are the right combination of rustic charm and modern luxury, making it an excellent choice for tourists seeking a one-of-a-kind vacation in Washington.

Snug Harbor, located on the west side of San Juan Island, offers elegant rustic décor in its cabins and suites, which include full kitchens and breathtaking views of Mitchell Bay. The towering ceilings and continuous vistas provide a sense of openness and closeness to the peaceful natural surroundings.

Snug Harbor Resort is a hidden gem for anyone seeking tranquility in the San Juan Islands.
The resort provides complimentary use of paddleboards, kayaks, canoes, and bikes, enabling visitors to discover the bay's beauties. For boating aficionados, there is also a private marina where you may dock throughout your visit.

Mitchell Bay Coffee Shop at the resort is a quiet place to start the day with a cup of coffee and some local delicacies. The gift shop, loaded with local items, adds to the allure of this quiet retreat. Whether you're sitting by the lake, creating a fire, or admiring the animals, Snug Harbor Resort provides a peaceful respite from the daily grind.

Snug Harbor Resort, with its spectacular scenery and plethora of amenities, is one of the finest places to stay in Washington for people looking for a calm and gorgeous vacation in the San Juan Islands.

## Frequently Asked Questions (FAQs) about the Most Unique Places to Stay in Washington State

Are you seeking additional information about places to stay in Washington State?
Here are some frequently asked questions (and answers) concerning Washington State's most distinctive hotels.

### Where are the greatest places to stay in Washington State?

The greatest spot to stay in Washington State is ultimately determined by your preferences. If you enjoy city life and culture, staying in downtown Seattle at hotels such as the Inn at the Market or The Edgewater is ideal. For nature enthusiasts, TreeHouse Point in Seattle and Carson Ridge Cabins in the Columbia River Gorge provide tranquil, natural settings. If you want to have a genuinely unique experience, stay aboard the Sleepless in Seattle Houseboat or the Anderson School Hotel in Bothell.

### Is Seattle a walkable city?

Absolutely! Seattle is an excellent city for walking. Pike Place Market, Belltown, and Capitol Hill are all excellent walking neighborhoods. You can simply walk around the downtown area, harbor, and various parks.

Furthermore, strolling is an excellent opportunity to discover the city's hidden beauties, such as charming cafés and interesting stores.

When planning a vacation to Washington State, think about what kind of experience you want to have and look into the different and great lodgings.

When planning a vacation to Washington State, think about what kind of experience you want to have and look into the different and great lodgings.

**What is the greatest time of year to visit Washington?**

Summer (June to August) is considered the greatest season to visit Washington State, particularly if you want to conduct outdoor activities. The weather is mild and mainly dry, ideal for hiking, sightseeing, and visiting national parks. However, for those who prefer fewer crowds and don't mind a little rain, spring (April to June) and fall (September to October) are also excellent times to come, with the added benefit of stunning spring blossoms and fall foliage.

**Is it pricey in Washington state?**

The cost varies greatly depending on where you travel and what you do. Seattle, as a big city, may be expensive, particularly in terms of lodging and restaurants. However, there are some low-cost choices accessible, such as inexpensive restaurants and free activities like parks and museums. Outside of Seattle, in areas such as the Olympic Peninsula or the Cascade Mountains, prices might be lower, particularly if you enjoy camping or staying in more primitive hotels.

## How far is Downtown Seattle from the airport?

Downtown Seattle is approximately 14 miles (22.5 kilometers) north of Seattle-Tacoma International Airport (SEA).

The trip typically takes 20-30 minutes, depending on traffic. Alternatively, you may ride the Link light rail, which is a convenient and inexpensive choice. The light rail operates every 6 to 15 minutes and takes around 40 minutes to reach downtown Seattle from the airport.

## Recap of Washington State's Unique Places to Stay

Finally, if I had to select one site in Washington State that genuinely catches my heart, it would be TreeHouse Point. There's something beautiful about waking up among the trees, totally immersed in nature yet still being near to the city. It's a rare combination of rustic charm and tranquility that can't be found anywhere else. If you're seeking a romantic weekend or a single retreat to refresh, this location provides a unique experience. Furthermore, being only a short drive from Seattle allows you to enjoy both tranquil nature and exciting city life.

So, if you're planning a vacation to Washington State, think about the type of experience you're looking for, and don't be afraid to explore the state's variety and excellent lodgings!

The greatest locations to stay in Washington State for each kind of traveler

**Did you like reading about places to stay in Washington state?**
Enjoy your stay ●

# Conclusion

As we complete our trip through "The Ultimate Washington Bucket List," we reflect on the Evergreen State's rich tapestry of experiences. Washington is more than simply a destination; it's a dynamic story of natural beauty, cultural variety, and historical significance waiting to be discovered and treasured.

From the foggy beaches of Puget Sound to the undulating hills of the Palouse, each region of Washington has its distinct narrative to tell. We've traveled through lively marketplaces, ascended high above the city in the Space Needle, and felt the pulse of a city that perfectly mixes the modern and traditional. The city's coffee culture, a reflection of its inventive spirit, entices visitors to linger in the quaint cafes that dot its vibrant districts.

Beyond the metropolitan attraction, Washington's natural landscapes provide a haven for the spirit. The Olympic Peninsula's rich rainforests and jagged shoreline demonstrate the state's biological variety. The beautiful Mount Rainier and the tranquil Cascade Range beckon explorers and nature lovers alike, providing hiking, skiing, and the opportunity to withdraw from the world and reconnect with nature.

In Eastern Washington, the narrative turns to a sun-drenched tapestry of vineyards and orchards. The Yakima Valley and Walla Walla districts provide more than simply wine tasting; they also allow visitors to witness the craftsmanship and attention that goes into each bottle. The link between land and people is evident here, and visitors are treated like friends rather than tourists.

Washington has a diverse cultural heritage. Its Native American roots, pioneering past, and many immigrant cultures have formed a state that is truly American yet also marvelously international. This diversity is reflected in its cuisine, festivals, and arts, resulting in a thriving cultural landscape with something for everyone.

Don't forget about the state's smaller towns and hidden jewels. Places like Leavenworth, with its Bavarian beauty, and the San Juan Islands, which provide an exquisite retreat from the mainland, all contribute to the state's attractiveness. Washington's picturesque byways, such as the majestic Chuckanut Drive and the historic Columbia River Highway, provide excursions as enjoyable as the attractions themselves.

As you finish this book, remember that the ultimate Washington bucket list is more than just a list of places; it's a beginning point for your trip to this amazing state. Whether you desire serenity in nature, the thrill of metropolitan discovery, or the warmth of small-town friendliness, Washington will welcome you with open arms and limitless options. Each visit, walk, dawn over the mountains, or sunset by the shore, adds another dimension to your comprehension and enjoyment of this unique and stunning state.

So pack your luggage, plan your schedule, and start on an adventure that promises to be both enlightening and thrilling. Washington awaits, eager to be a part of your journey and provide experiences that will stay with you long after you return home.

*Thank you for following my trip through "The Ultimate Washington Bucket List." I hope this guide inspires you to explore the Evergreen State and enriches your travels with unique encounters.*

# Bonus

## *10  Free Washington bucket list Travel planner*

### Washington bucket list Travel Journal

Date:                              Transport:

Weather          🌥  ☀  💧  🌙  ❄

| Note for side attraction | Places: |
|---|---|
| Here you can record lovely things seen in Washington | |

Notes

# Washington bucket list Travel Journal

Date: _____     Transport: _____

Weather  🐢  ☀  💧  ☾  ❄

| Note for side attraction | Places: |
|---|---|

Here you can record lovely
things seen in Washington

Notes

# Washington bucket list Travel Journal

Date:                    Transport:

Weather

## Note for side attraction

Here you can record lovely
things seen in Washington

## Places:

## Notes

# Washington bucket list Travel Journal

Date: _____     Transport: _____

Weather     🐑  ☀️  💧  🌙  ❄️

| Note for side attraction | Places: |
|---|---|

Here you can record lovely
things seen in Washington

Notes

# Washington bucket list Travel Journal

Date: _____    Transport: _____

Weather ☁ ☀ ☂ ☾ ❄

## Note for side attraction

Here you can record lovely things seen in Washington

## Places:

## Notes

# Washington bucket list Travel Journal

Date: _____ Transport: _____

Weather

| Note for side attraction | Places: |
|---|---|

Here you can record lovely
things seen in Washington

Notes

# *Washington bucket list Travel Journal*

Date: _____          Transport: _____

Weather          🐢     ☀️     💧     🌙     ❄️

| Note for side attraction | Places: |
|---|---|

Here you can record lovely things seen in Washington

Notes

# Washington bucket list Travel Journal

Date: _____        Transport: _____

Weather

| Note for side attraction | Places: |
|---|---|

Here you can record lovely
things seen in Washington

Notes

# Washington bucket list Travel Journal

Date: _____ Transport: _____

Weather

## Note for side attraction

Here you can record lovely things seen in Washington

## Places:

## Notes

# Washington bucket list Travel Journal

Date: _____     Transport: _____

Weather ☀ 💧 🌙 ❄

| Note for side attraction | Places: |
|---|---|

Here you can record lovely things seen in Washington

Notes

Made in United States
Troutdale, OR
02/13/2024

17657722R00086